**HBR'S
10
MUST
READS**

# On
**Innovation**

HBR's 10 Must Reads series is the definitive collection of ideas and best practices for aspiring and experienced leaders alike. These books offer essential reading selected from the pages of *Harvard Business Review* on topics critical to the success of every manager.

**Titles include:**

HBR's 10 Must Reads on Change Management
HBR's 10 Must Reads on Collaboration
HBR's 10 Must Reads on Communication
HBR's 10 Must Reads on Innovation
HBR's 10 Must Reads on Leadership
HBR's 10 Must Reads on Making Smart Decisions
HBR's 10 Must Reads on Managing People
HBR's 10 Must Reads on Managing Yourself
HBR's 10 Must Reads on Strategic Marketing
HBR's 10 Must Reads on Strategy
HBR's 10 Must Reads on Teams
HBR's 10 Must Reads: The Essentials

# On
# Innovation

**HARVARD BUSINESS REVIEW PRESS**
Boston, Massachusetts

The web addresses referenced in this book were live and correct at the time of
book's publication but may be subject to change.

Library of Congress Cataloging-in-Publication Data

HBR's 10 must reads on innovation.
   pages cm
  Includes index.
   ISBN 978-1-4221-8985-6 (alk. paper)
   1. Creative ability in business.   2. Creative thinking.   3. Diffusion of
innovations—Management.   4. Technological innovations—Management.
5. New products.   I. Harvard business review   II. Title: HBR's ten must reads
on innovation.
   HD53.H394 2013
   658.4'063—dc23

                                                          2012045970

The paper used in this publication meets the requirements of the American
National Standard for Permanence of Paper for Publications and Documents in
Libraries and Archives Z39.48-1992.

# Contents

**HBR'S 10 MUST READS**

# On
# **Innovation**

# The Innovation Catalysts

*by Roger L. Martin*

**ONE DAY IN 2007,** midway through a five-hour PowerPoint presentation, Scott Cook realized that he wasn't another Steve Jobs. At first it was a bitter disappointment. Like many entrepreneurs, Cook wanted the company he had cofounded to be like Apple—design driven, innovation intensive, wowing consumers year in and year out with fantastic offerings. But that kind of success always seemed to need a powerful visionary at the top.

This article is about how Cook and his colleagues at the software development company Intuit found an alternative to the Steve Jobs model: one that has enabled Intuit to become a design-driven innovation machine. Any corporation—no matter how small or prosaic its business—can make the same grassroots transformation if it really wants to.

## The Birth of the Idea

Intuit's transformation arguably began in 2004, with its adoption of the famous Net Promoter Score. Developed by Fred Reichheld, of Bain & Company, NPS depends on one simple question for customers: How likely are you, on a scale of 0 (not at all likely) to 10 (extremely likely), to recommend this product or service to a colleague or friend? "Detractors" answer from 0 to 6, "passives" answer 7 or 8, and "promoters" answer 9 or 10. A company's Net Promoter Score is the percentage of promoters less the percentage of detractors.

For the first couple of years, Intuit saw its NPS rise significantly, owing to a number of marketing initiatives. But by 2007 NPS growth had stalled. It was not hard to see why. Although Intuit had lowered its detractor percentage substantially, it had made little headway with promoters. Customer recommendations of new products were especially disappointing.

Clearly, Intuit needed to figure out how to galvanize its customers. Cook, a member of Procter & Gamble's board of directors, approached Claudia Kotchka, then P&G's vice president of design innovation and strategy, for advice. Following their discussions, Cook and Steve Bennett, then Intuit's CEO, decided to focus on the role of design in innovation at a two-day off-site for the company's top 300 managers. Cook created a one-day program on what he called Design for Delight (D4D)—an event aimed at launching Intuit's reinvention as a design-driven company.

The centerpiece of the day was that five-hour PowerPoint presentation, in which Cook laid out the wonders of design and how it could entice Intuit's customers. The managers listened dutifully and clapped appreciatively at the end, as they were supposed to; Cook was, after all, a company founder. Nevertheless, he was disappointed by his reception. Despite some interest in the ideas presented, there was little energy in the room.

But although the main event fell flat, the one that followed did not. Cook had met a young consulting associate professor at Stanford named Alex Kazaks, whom he'd invited to present for an hour at the off-site. Like Cook, Kazaks began with a PowerPoint presentation, but he ended his after 10 minutes and used the rest of the time for a participatory exercise: The managers worked through a design challenge, creating prototypes, getting feedback, iterating, and refining.

The group was mesmerized. Afterward Cook informally polled the participants, asking what takeaways they'd gotten from the daylong session. Two-thirds of the lessons they reported came from

# Idea in Brief

A few years ago the software development company Intuit realized that it needed a new approach to galvanizing customers. The company's Net Promoter Score was faltering, and customer recommendations of new products were especially disappointing. Intuit decided to hold a two-day, off-site meeting for the company's top 300 managers with a focus on the role of design in innovation. One of the days was dedicated to a program called Design for Delight. The centerpiece of the day was a PowerPoint presentation by Intuit founder Scott Cook, who realized midway through that he was no Steve Jobs: The managers listened dutifully, but there was little energy in the room. By contrast, a subsequent exercise in which the

participants worked through a design challenge by creating prototypes, getting feedback, iterating, and refining, had them mesmerized. The eventual result was the creation of a team of nine design-thinking coaches—"innovation catalysts"—from across Intuit who were made available to help any work group create prototypes, run experiments, and learn from customers. The process includes a "painstorm" (to determine the customer's greatest pain point), a "sol-jam" (to generate and then winnow possible solutions), and a "code-jam" (to write code "good enough" to take to customers within two weeks). Design for Delight has enabled employees throughout Intuit to move from satisfying customers to delighting them.

the hands-on exercise. This reaction made Cook think: He might not be the next Steve Jobs, but perhaps his company didn't need one. Given a few tools, coaching, and practice, could the grass roots of the company drive success in innovation and customer delight?

## From Idea to Initiative

Like most Silicon Valley tech companies, Intuit had user-interface designers, graphic designers, and others buried relatively deep in the organization. Cook turned to a particularly talented young design director, Kaaren Hanson, and asked her what she would do to promote design at Intuit.

Hanson realized that the company needed an organized program for moving from talking about D4D to doing it. She persuaded Cook to let her create a team of design-thinking coaches—"innovation catalysts"—who could help Intuit managers work on initiatives throughout the organization. Hanson selected nine colleagues to join her in this role. Their training and deployment was her central agenda for FY 2009.

In selecting the nine, Hanson looked first for people with a broad perspective on what it meant to be a designer: Beyond creating a graphic user interface that was both appealing and intuitive, it included thinking about whether the software solved the user's problem in a delightful way. She wanted her coaches to be interested in talking to users and solving problems with colleagues rather than depending solely on their own genius. If they were to successfully coach others in design thinking, they'd need an outgoing personality and good people skills.

She invited two direct reports from her own business unit and seven people from other units across the company. The group included six women and four men. They came from a variety of fields within Intuit—design, research, product management—and had titles such as user-interface architect, principal researcher, staff designer, and product manager. Hanson chose people who were influential even though they were all one or two levels below director, meaning closer to the bottom of the organization than the top. All nine signed up enthusiastically.

To begin building design thinking into the DNA of the company, Cook and Hanson organized a series of Design for Delight forums. These were typically attended by more than 1,000 employees and featured a speaker who'd had exemplary success in creating customer delight. Half the featured speakers came from inside Intuit; the other half included the founding CEO of Flip Video, Facebook's top data scientist, and the head of Apple Stores. The forums also showcased D4D successes to date and shared best practices. People who worked together were encouraged to attend together and were asked as a team to identify the one thing they would do differently after the forum.

To ensure that managers who were thinking design didn't become too intimidated to begin the process, or frustrated trying to do something with which they had little experience, or delayed by needing to hire an outside design consultant, Hanson's innovation catalysts were available to help any work group create prototypes, run experiments, and learn from customers. Of course, there was a risk that this would stretch the catalysts too thin, so Hanson placed some constraints on their availability. They were expected to spend 25% of their time on big-payoff projects for Intuit overall. Hanson kept in close contact with general managers who had catalysts working with them to make sure that the catalysts were addressing the managers' biggest problems. She realized that if design momentum was to be maintained, her coaches had to be seen as responsible for three or four visible and high-impact wins a year.

Some enabling came from the very bottom of the organization. In 2008 two employees who had been at Intuit only four months designed an online social network for the D4D initiative, which they rolled out the following year with management's consent but without its direct support. In its first year the new platform, named Brainstorm, generated 32 ideas that made it to market.

## From Presentations to Experiments

Traditionally, decisions at Intuit had been made on the basis of PowerPoint presentations. Managers would work to produce both (what they saw as) a great product and a great presentation for selling the concept to their bosses. Under this system Intuit managers voted on ideas and then tried to sell them to customers. A key component of D4D, therefore, was shifting the focus away from managerial presentations. It would be far better, Hanson and Cook realized, to learn directly from customers through experiments.

Today D4D innovations begin with what Intuit calls the painstorm—a process developed by two innovation catalysts, Rachel Evans and Kim McNealy. It is aimed at figuring out customers' greatest pain point for which Intuit can provide relief.

# Recruiting the Innovation Catalysts

**IN 2008 KAAREN HANSON** sent this e-mail to some Intuit colleagues:

### Subject: Phase II of Design for Delight—we need YOU

You have been nominated (and your participation has been approved by your manager) to help us drive Phase II of Design for Delight at Intuit. You are a critical leader who can enable Intuit to become one of the principal design-thinking cultures. We have a number of levers at our disposal but we need your help to develop even better ideas to drive design thinking deeper into the organization.

Here's what you'll be committing to:

- **Actively participate in a one-day brainstorm/workshop** in early August to work through what we (as a force of design thinking and as a larger company) might do to take Design for Delight to its next level. Scott will come by and respond to our ideas/plan towards the end of the day

- **Commit to the execution of initiatives** generated through the August workshop

- **Become a more visible Design for Delight leader** across Intuit (e.g., help teach a Design for Delight 101 session/workshop to FastPath or some other such leadership session, contribute to the D4D body of knowledge through existing and future contribution systems, be a sounding board for Intuit execs)

- **Be a D4D coach/facilitator** that the larger company can draw upon (e.g., coach key teams across Intuit in brainstorming, design reviews, etc.)

In total, your commitment will be about 2 days/month—and we'll be able to work around your schedule.

Let me know if you are in for FY09—and I'll get the August date on everyone's calendars. Right now, we're looking at an in-person workshop on August 4th, 5th, or 6th in Mountain View.

---

In a painstorm, team members talk to and observe customers in their offices or homes rather than sit in Intuit offices and imagine what they want. This exercise often shatters preconceptions. Going into one painstorm for a sales-oriented product, the team was convinced that the product concept should be "Grow your business."

But the painstorm showed that "Grow your business" sounded very ambiguous to customers—it could refer to growing revenues from their existing customers (not a pain point for them) or to acquiring similar small businesses (also not a pain point, but expensive). The true pain point was acquiring entirely new customers through organic sales efforts. "Get customers" was a winning concept that focused laserlike on that.

Next, within two weeks, the group holds a "sol-jam," in which people generate concepts for as many product or service solutions as possible to address the pain points they've identified and then weed the concepts down to a short list for prototyping and testing. In the early days of prototyping, these high-potential solutions were integrated into Intuit's software development process. But the innovation catalysts realized that the best way to maintain momentum would be to get code into users' hands as quickly as possible. This would help determine whether the solution had potential and, if so, what needed to be done to enhance it. So the third step became moving immediately to "code-jam," with the goal of writing code that wasn't airtight but was good enough to take to customers within two weeks of the sol-jam. Thus, proceeding from the painstorm to the first user feedback on a new product usually takes only four weeks.

Let's look at a couple of examples. When Intuit's tax group began to think about mobile apps, Carol Howe, a project manager and innovation catalyst, started with the customer. Her five-person team went "out in the wild," she says, to observe dozens of smartphone users. It quickly narrowed in on millennials, whose income range made them likely candidates for the simplest tax experience. The team created multiple concepts and iterated with customers on a weekly basis. They brought customers in each Friday, distilled what they'd learned on Monday, brainstormed concepts on Tuesday, designed them on Wednesday, and coded them on Thursday, before bringing the customers in again. Through these iterations the team uncovered multiple "delighters." They launched a pilot in California in January 2010 and expanded nationwide in January 2011. The resulting application, SnapTax, has 4.5 stars in both the Apple and Android stores and a Net Promoter Score in the high 80s.

An even better example comes from India. In 2008 members of the India team came up with an idea remote from tax preparation and other core Intuit North America products, none of which were likely to succeed in India. The idea, a service for poor Indian farmers, was interesting enough for Intuit to give Deepa Bachu, a longtime development manager, the green light to explore it. Bachu and an engineer spent weeks following subsistence farmers through their daily lives—in the fields, in their villages, and at the markets where they sold their produce. The two came to appreciate the farmers' greatest pain point—perishable inventory that either went unsold or got a suboptimal price. If Intuit could enable the farmers to consistently sell their produce before spoilage and at a decent price, their pain would be reduced or eliminated.

After the painstorm and the sol-jam, the team went into rapid experimentation. Within seven weeks it was running a test of what was eventually launched as Mobile Bazaar, a simple text-messaging-based marketplace connecting buyers and sellers. To get there so fast, the team had cleverly faked parts of the product that would have been costly and slow to code and build. These came to be known as "fako backends." What the user saw looked real, but behind the user interface was a human being—like the Wizard of Oz behind the curtain—rather than thousands of lines of code that would have taken months to write.

The initial trials showed that half the farmers were able to increase their prices by more than 10%; some of them earned as much as 50% more. Within a year of launch, Mobile Bazaar had 180,000 subscribing farmers, most of them acquired by word of mouth. They report that, on average, the service boosts their prices by 16%.

## From Breakthroughs to Culture

Hanson was pleased with the progress of the 10 original innovation catalysts in their first year and with the organization's receptivity, but she knew that Intuit would have to scale up to make the transformation complete. Brad Smith, the new CEO, was raising innovation expectations for the whole company, focusing particularly on new arenas that he described as "mobile, social, and global." Hanson set a goal for FY 2010 to select, train, and deploy another 65 catalysts. This meant sourcing from a broader pool of talent—going deeper into product management and engineering—and creating a small dedicated team to support the catalysts and increase D4D pull from midlevel managers.

She appointed Suzanne Pellican, one of the original 10, to expand the catalysts' number and capabilities. Hanson had learned from the initial work that the strongest design thinkers didn't necessarily make the best catalysts. She says, "We not only needed people who were design thinkers—we also needed people with passion to give D4D away and help others to do great work, versus coming up with a great idea and bringing it to others."

The catalysts also needed mutual support. Hanson's team had found that they did their best work when they worked together. They learned new ideas and techniques from one another and provided moral support in tough situations. So as Pellican scaled up the catalyst corps, she made sure that each catalyst was part of an organized "posse" that typically extended across business units, allowing new methods to travel quickly from one end of the organization to the other.

To increase the catalysts' effectiveness, Hanson established a second small team—led by Joseph O'Sullivan, another of the original 10—to help middle management embrace both design thinking as a concept and the innovation catalysts as enablers. For example, after several catalysts reported encountering resistance at the director level, Hanson and O'Sullivan worked to integrate design thinking into Intuit's leadership training programs, applying it directly to problems that leaders faced. In one training program an IT director was challenged to lead a team tasked with reducing company spending on employees' mobile devices by $500,000. O'Sullivan's group held a one-day session on painstorming and sol-jamming for the team. The IT director achieved the desired saving and won much appreciation from the members of her team for having made their task so much easier than expected. She and the other participants in that leadership training program became fervent D4D advocates.

---

**Encouraging experimentation** rather than PowerPoint has enabled employees throughout Intuit to move from satisfying customers to delighting them. Design for Delight has stuck because people see that it is an obviously better and more enjoyable way of innovating.

Innovation activity has increased dramatically in the organization. Take TurboTax, Intuit's single biggest product. In the 2006 tax year the TurboTax unit ran just one customer experiment. In 2010 it ran 600. Experiments in the QuickBooks unit went from a few each year to 40 last year. Intuit now seizes new opportunities more quickly. Brad Smith pushed for D4D-led innovation in the fast-growing arena of mobile apps, and within 24 months the company went from zero to 18, with a number of them, including SnapTax, off to a very successful start. Net Promoter Scores are up across the company, and growth in revenue and income has increased over the past three years.

Scott Cook may not have been another Steve Jobs, but it turned out that Intuit didn't need one.

**Originally published in June 2011.  Reprint R1106E**

# Stop the Innovation Wars

*by Vijay Govindarajan and Chris Trimble*

**IT WAS JUST AN INNOCENT COMMENT.** While working with a client at a *Fortune* 500 company, we proposed the formation of a special group to execute a new growth strategy. "For now, let's just refer to the group as the innovation team," we suggested.

The client rolled his eyes. "Let's call it anything but that," he said. "What is this so-called innovation team going to do? Brainstorm? Sit around being creative all day? Talk condescendingly about a superior organizational culture? All of this while operating with neither discipline nor accountability? All of this while the rest of us get the real work done?"

Wow. All it took was two words: *innovation team*.

In our experience, innovation teams feel a hostility toward the people responsible for day-to-day operations that is just as biting. The rich vocabulary of disdain includes *bureaucratic, robotic, rigid, ossified, staid, dull, decaying, controlling, patronizing* . . . and just plain *old*. Such animosity explains why most executives believe that any significant innovation initiative requires a team that is separate and isolated from the rest of the company.

But that conventional wisdom is worse than simpleminded. It is flat wrong. Isolation may neutralize infighting, but it also neuters innovation.

The reality is that an innovation initiative must be executed by a partnership that somehow bridges the hostilities—a partnership between a dedicated team and what we call the *performance engine,* the unit responsible for sustaining excellence in ongoing operations. Granted, such an arrangement seems, at first glance, improbable. But to give up on it is to give up on innovation itself. Almost all innovation initiatives build directly upon a company's existing resources and know-how—brands, customer relationships, manufacturing capabilities, technical expertise, and so forth. So when a large corporation asks a group to innovate in isolation, it not only ends up duplicating things it already has but also forfeits its primary advantage over smaller, nimbler rivals—its mammoth asset base.

Over the past decade, we have examined dozens of innovation initiatives and identified some best practices. In the process we built upon foundational management theories such as Jim March's ideas about balancing exploration with exploitation, and Paul Lawrence and Jay Lorsch's argument that firms need to both integrate and differentiate corporate units. We came to the conclusion that the organizational model we prescribe—a partnership between a dedicated team and the performance engine—is surprisingly versatile. It can be adapted to initiatives that span many innovation categories—sustaining and disruptive; incremental and radical; competence enhancing and competence destroying; new processes, new products, new businesses, and high-risk new ventures.

This article will show how to make the unlikeliest partnership work. There are three steps. First, decide which tasks the performance engine can handle and which you'll need to hand off to a dedicated team. Second, assemble the right dedicated team. Third, anticipate and mitigate strains in the partnership. Once you have taken these steps, you'll be in a good position to actually execute on your great ideas.

## How One Company Organized for Growth

In most law offices, even in the internet era, you'll find libraries full of weighty and majestic-looking books. The books contain rulings from past cases. With each verdict, judges contribute to a massive body of precedents that shape future decisions. (This is the system,

# Idea in Brief

Special teams dedicated to innovation initiatives inevitably run into conflict with the rest of the organization. The people responsible for ongoing operations view the innovators as undisciplined upstarts. The innovators dismiss the operations people as bureaucratic dinosaurs. It's natural to separate the two warring groups. But it's also dead wrong, say Tuck Business School's Govindarajan and Trimble. Nearly all innovation initiatives build on a firm's existing resources and know-how. When a group is asked to innovate in isolation, the corporation forfeits its main advantage over smaller, nimbler rivals—its mammoth asset base. The best approach is to set up a partnership between the dedicated team and the people who maintain excellence in ongoing operations,

the company's performance engine. Such partnerships were key to the successful launch of new offerings by legal publisher Westlaw, Lucent Technologies, and WD-40. There are three steps to making the partnership work: First, decide which tasks the performance engine can handle, assigning it only those that flow along the same path as ongoing operations. Next, assemble a dedicated team to carry out the rest, being careful to bring in outside perspectives and create new norms. Last, proactively manage conflicts. The key here is having an innovation leader who can collaborate well with the performance engine and a senior executive who supports the dedicated team, prioritizes the company's long-term interests, and adjudicates contests for resources.

at least, in the United States and many other countries.) Law students spend countless hours mastering the intricacies and subtleties of researching precedents.

West, a 135-year-old business, is one of several publishing houses whose mission is to make legal research easier. After it was acquired by the Thomson Corporation, now Thomson Reuters, in 1996, West experienced five years of double-digit growth, as the industry made a rapid transition from printed books to online databases. But in 2001 a major problem arose. Once nearly all of West's customers had converted to Westlaw, the company's online offering, West's growth plummeted to near zero.

To restart growth, West set its sights on expanding its product line. By studying its customers—law firms, corporate law offices,

# Questions to Ask

### When Dividing the Labor

1. Does my company already have the needed skills for all aspects of the project?

2. What portions of the innovation initiative are consistent with the existing work relationships in the performance engine?

### When Assembling the Dedicated Team

1. What is the right mix of insiders and outsiders?

2. How should the team be structured differently from the performance engine?

3. How should the team be measured and incentivized?

### As You Manage the Strains on the Partnership

1. Is there a tone of mutual respect?

2. Are resource conflicts resolved proactively?

3. Is the shared staff giving sufficient attention to the innovation initiative?

---

and law schools, among others—and how they worked, West saw that lawyers had no convenient access to many key sources of information. For example, to examine legal strategies in past cases, law firms were sending runners to courthouses to dig through dusty archives and photocopy old briefs—documents written by lawyers for judges, often to summarize their arguments.

Starting with an online database of briefs, West proceeded to launch a series of new digital products. By 2007, West had restored its organic growth to nearly 7% annually—quite an accomplishment since its customer base was growing much more slowly.

An expansion into databases for different kinds of documents does not seem, at first glance, as if it would have been a stretch for West. But Mike Wilens, then the CEO, and his head of product development, Erv Barbre, immediately saw that the briefs project, because of its size, complexity, and unfamiliarity, was beyond the capabilities of West's performance engine. Some kind of special team was needed. At the same time, Wilens and Barbre were confident that portions of the project could be tackled by West's existing staff. They just had to make sure the two groups worked well together. Ultimately, the new briefs offering succeeded because Wilens and Barbre built an effective partnership between a dedicated team and the performance engine, following the three steps we've outlined.

## Divide the Labor

Step one in forming the partnership is to define the responsibilities of each partner. Naturally, you want to assign as much as you can to the performance engine. It already exists and works well. But caution is due. You need to realistically assess what the performance engine can handle while it maintains excellence in ongoing operations.

The proper division of labor can span a wide range—from 10/90, to 50/50, to 90/10 splits. It depends on the nature of the initiative and the performance engine's capabilities. So how do you decide?

The performance engine has two essential limitations. The first is straightforward. Any task that is beyond the capabilities of the individuals within the performance engine must be assigned to the dedicated team. The second limitation is less obvious. It involves work relationships. What Person A and Person B can do together is not just a function of A's skills and B's skills. It is also a function of the way A and B are accustomed to working together. As long as A and B are working inside the performance engine, their work relationship is extremely difficult to change. It is reinforced daily by the demands of ongoing operations. BMW was confronted with this second limitation when it designed its first hybrid vehicle. (See the sidebar "Why BMW Didn't Reinvent the Wheel.")

Therefore, the performance engine should take on only tasks that flow along the same path from person to person that ongoing operations do—at the same pace and with the same people in charge. To ask more of the performance engine is too disruptive. It embeds conflicts between innovation and ongoing operations so deeply within the performance engine that they become impossible to manage.

## Case Study: Why BMW Didn't Reinvent the Wheel

**AT THE HEART OF EVERY HYBRID** automobile lies a regenerative brake. Traditional brakes dissipate the energy produced by a vehicle's motion, generating friction and useless heat. Regenerative brakes, by contrast, capture the energy and put it back to work. An electrical generator built into the brake recharges the hybrid's massive batteries as the car slows.

Chris Bangle, then chief of design at BMW, was discouraged by slow progress early in the company's first effort to design a hybrid vehicle, launched in 2007. The source of the problem, Bangle saw, had nothing to do with engineering prowess; BMW employed the right experts. The problem lay in the company's formal structure and processes. Under its well-established design procedures, there was no reason for battery specialists to speak with brake specialists. There was no routine work flow between them.

Bangle ultimately decided to create a dedicated team to enable the deep collaboration that was necessary among all component specialists involved in the regenerative brake design. He named it the "energy chain" team, and it succeeded in moving the project forward quickly. Although a dedicated team was required for this one aspect of vehicle design, all other aspects of BMW's first hybrid launch—design, engineering, sales, marketing, distribution, and so forth—were handled by its performance engine.

---

At West, Wilens and Barbre recognized that although product development staffers had deep expertise in judicial decisions—such as *Miranda v. Arizona, Brown v. Board of Education, Roe v. Wade,* and thousands more—they had no experience in gathering briefs, which were scattered throughout countless courthouses and were much harder to track and organize than decisions were. A complicating factor was scale. There can be dozens of briefs for every judicial decision. The dedicated team, at the very least, had to take responsibility for locating and acquiring the briefs—and would need a few outside experts to be effective.

More critically, Wilens and Barbre saw that the briefs project as a whole would be inconsistent with the work relationships within West's product development group. Composed of about 50 legal experts, the group worked on a few dozen small initiatives at a time. The typical project was an improvement to the Westlaw database that involved only two or three people for up to a few weeks. The group was nonhierarchical, and the individuals within it did not depend heavily on one another. In fact, during a given project, a product developer's most important work relationship was likely to be cross-functional, with a peer in the information technology group.

The briefs project was much larger. At its peak, it involved 30 people full-time. The product developers needed to work together in an unfamiliar manner. Each needed to take on a specialized role as part of a tightly structured, close-knit project team. Asking the developers to operate in both modes at once would have been disruptive and confusing for all involved. Therefore Wilens and Barbre assigned nearly the entire product development task to a dedicated team.

However, they assigned the marketing and sales tasks to the performance engine. Marketing and selling briefs was not much different from marketing and selling Westlaw. The buyers were the same, and the value proposition was easy to explain. The work could simply be added to West's existing marketing and sales processes. It would flow along the same path, at the same pace, and with the same people in charge. The sales and marketing teams were a component of the performance engine that could do double duty—a subset we refer to as the *shared staff*.

## Assemble the Dedicated Team

Once the labor has been divided and the required skill sets have been identified, the principles for assembling the dedicated team are uncomplicated. First, choose the best people you can get, from any source (internal transfers, external hires, even small acquisitions). Then, organize the team in a way that makes the most sense for the task at hand. Tackle the process as if you were building a new company from the ground up. This was the approach Lucent took in launching a new unit that quickly grew to $2 billion in annual revenues. (See the sidebar "Why Lucent Engineered a Service Business from Scratch.")

Alas, these principles are easy to state but extremely difficult to follow. Companies have a pernicious habit of creating subunits that behave just like the rest of the company, as though a genetic code

## Case Study: Why Lucent Engineered a Service Business from Scratch

**IN 2006, LUCENT SIGNED** a deal to help a major telecommunications company transform its network. Four years earlier, such a huge service deal would have been hard to imagine.

Lucent's historical strength was in products and in making technological breakthroughs in telecommunications hardware. But after the dot-com bust, Lucent needed a new source of growth and looked to services.

While the company had the necessary technical skills for services, it hardly had the organizational DNA. Technologists, not client relationship managers, held most of the power. And the pace of service operations was week to week, a stark departure from telecom hardware purchasing cycles, which lasted years. As such, Lucent recognized that nearly the entire project needed to be executed by a dedicated team.

Lucent assembled that team as if it were building a new company. It hired an outside leader, a veteran of services from EDS, and several experienced service executives. It adopted new HR policies that mimicked those of service companies. And it created a new performance scorecard, one that emphasized workforce utilization, not product line ROI. It even tied compensation for service deliverers directly to their utilization rates. The result? In four years' time, Lucent's service group was generating more than $2 billion in revenues.

---

has been passed from parent to offspring. We think of such subunits as *little performance engines,* and they quickly bring innovation initiatives to a standstill.

The most frequent source of the problem is the instinct to populate dedicated teams entirely with insiders. This is understandable. It's natural to think about who you know before thinking about skills you need. Insiders are easy to find, often cheaper to "hire," and seem less risky because they're known commodities. They also offer a critical benefit: Because of their familiarity with the organization and credibility within it, they can help mitigate conflicts between the dedicated team and the performance engine.

The trouble is that a dedicated team composed entirely of insiders is practically guaranteed to act like a little performance engine. For one thing, everyone has the same biases and instincts, grounded in the history of a single company. Furthermore, work relationships are sticky. As noted earlier, employees who have worked together for years have a hard time altering the way they interact.

Building an effective dedicated team requires breaking down existing work relationships and creating new ones. Including some outsiders, even just one in three, is a powerful expedient. Outsiders have no existing work relationships to break down. They must form new ones from scratch. As a bonus, outsiders naturally challenge assumptions because their biases and instincts are rooted in the experiences of other companies.

Managers can also accelerate the process of breaking down and re-creating work relationships by writing new job descriptions, inventing new and unfamiliar titles, and explicitly shifting the balance of power within the team. Shifting that balance is important because it is rarely the case that a company's traditional power center (say, engineering) should also dominate the dedicated team (if, for example, customers for the innovation initiative will care more about a new product's look than its performance).

Selecting the right people and forming new work relationships are the foundational steps in building an effective dedicated team, but it is also important to pay attention to other forces that shape behaviors. Beyond new work relationships, dedicated teams frequently require performance metrics, incentives, and cultural norms that differ from those of the performance engine.

West built a dedicated team that was distinct from its existing product development staff, choosing a roughly 50/50 mix of insiders and outsiders. The company acquired a small business that had assembled on microfiche a collection of valuable briefs, including the very first brief filed before the U.S. Supreme Court. With it, West brought on board about a dozen people who knew a great deal about briefs and had no work relationships with the West team.

The leader of the briefs effort, Steve Anderson, treated the process of turning the mix of insiders and outsiders into a structured team as a zero-based effort. Rather than drawing on any of West's norms for how work gets done (who's responsible for what, who has what decision rights, and so forth), he simply gathered everyone and said, "Here we are. This is our task. How should we make it happen?"

Of course, the way to organize the effort was not obvious on day one. Innovation initiatives are ambiguous. As Anderson's team gained experience, its structure evolved. It's not essential that the dedicated team's structure be perfectly clear at the outset—only that it be unconstrained by the parent company's past.

Working on Anderson's dedicated team felt much different to the insiders who were part of it. They had less autonomy. They had to collaborate with peers much more closely. And they knew that if they stumbled, they would be letting down not just themselves but their teammates and their company. Some struggled with the transition and chose to return to the performance engine. While this may seem unfortunate, it was actually a mark of Anderson's success. As a general rule, if all the insiders on the dedicated team are comfortable, it must be a little performance engine. (Note that it's also important for insiders to have a clear path to get back to the performance engine. Innovation initiatives frequently fail, and the individuals working on them sometimes don't succeed in their assignments. Companies that create an out for insiders will find that they can more easily motivate people to join a dedicated team.)

To further shape his dedicated team, Anderson drew clear distinctions between its standards and cultural values and those of the performance engine. West had long maintained extremely high quality standards. For judicial decisions—literally, the law itself—customers demanded infallible information. Therefore, West had implemented multistep checks and safeguards in loading documents into its database, a process that often started with scanning a physical document. With briefs, however, West needed to relax, slightly, from being obsessive about quality to being diligent. The dauntingly high number of briefs made exhaustive precautions impractical. Besides, customers cared more about convenience and availability than perfection.

## Anticipate and Mitigate the Strains

Make no mistake, nurturing a healthy partnership is challenging. Conflicts between innovation initiatives and ongoing operations are normal and can easily escalate. Tensions become rivalries, rivalries become hostilities, and hostilities become all-out wars in which the company's long-term viability is the clearest loser.

Differences between the two groups run deep. Managers of the performance engine seek to be efficient, accountable, on time, on budget, and on spec. In every company, their basic approach is the same. It is to make every task, process, and activity as repeatable and predictable as possible. An innovation initiative, of course, is exactly the opposite. It is, by nature, nonroutine and uncertain. These incompatibilities create a natural us-versus-them dynamic.

Leaders must counter conflicts by constantly reinforcing a relationship of mutual respect. Dedicated team leaders must remember that profits from the performance engine pay for innovation, and that their success depends on their ability to leverage its assets. They must also remember that pushback from the performance engine does not arise from laziness or from an instinctive resistance to change. Quite the contrary—it arises from the efforts of good people doing good work, trying to run ongoing operations as effectively as possible. For their part, performance engine leaders must recognize that no performance engine lasts forever. To dismiss innovation leaders as reckless rebels intent on undermining discipline in the pursuit of an esoteric dream is to write off the company's future.

For the partnership to work, the leader of the innovation initiative must set the right tone—positive and collaborative. Antagonizing the performance engine is a *really bad* idea. The performance engine always wins in an all-out fight. It is, quite simply, bigger and stronger.

In fact, for precisely that reason, even the best innovation leaders need help from high places. They must be directly supported by an executive senior enough to act in the long-term interests of the company, overriding the performance engine's short-term demands when necessary. This typically means that the innovation leader must report two or more levels higher up than managers with budgets of a similar size. At WD-40, for example, an innovation initiative relied on the direct involvement of the CEO. (See "How WD-40 Minimized Frictions.")

The senior executive to whom the innovation leader reports must be careful not to be a cheerleader only for innovation. He or she

# Case Study: How WD-40 Minimized Frictions

**TO SPUR ORGANIC GROWTH,** Garry Ridge, CEO of WD-40, created a team to develop breakthrough products. He called it Team Tomorrow. It included newly hired research scientists and new outside partners. One of its first endeavors was developing the No-Mess Pen, which made it easy to dispense small quantities of WD-40 in tight spaces. Though it doesn't sound like a radical innovation, the technological challenges were steep, and the product took months to develop.

Historically, WD-40's marketing team had handled product development, which generally entailed routine efforts to improve, renew, or repackage existing products. Now marketing took on the responsibility of partnering with Team Tomorrow to commercialize its offerings.

The sources of conflict in this partnership are not hard to identify. First, some marketing staffers felt that the attractive challenge of developing breakthrough products should have been theirs. Then there was a resource constraint. Would the marketing team expend its limited time and resources on experimental products or proven performers? Finally, marketing worried that Team Tomorrow's new offerings would cannibalize existing products.

Graham Milner and Stephanie Barry, the leaders of Team Tomorrow, overcame these conflicts by taking a collaborative approach, particularly with

must also extol the virtues and importance of the performance engine and emphasize that a long-run victory for the company requires that both sides win.

Together, the innovation leader and the senior executive must anticipate and proactively resolve conflicts. The clashes can be intense, but if the labor is properly divided between the performance engine and the dedicated team, they'll be manageable. The most common conflict is over scarce resources. When the sum of activities, innovation plus ongoing operations, pushes the performance engine beyond its resource constraints, choices must be made.

Sometimes, this competition for scarce resources takes place through formal budgeting processes. Innovation leaders often find themselves seeking explicit commitments from multiple performance the head of marketing. They shared information, established an open-door policy, and coordinated plans carefully with marketing, anticipating bottlenecks and resource conflicts. Knowing that such conflicts could be resolved only by the CEO, Milner and Barry made sure Ridge was aware of them early, so that he could set priorities. When Ridge saw that it was necessary, he added staff to the marketing team to make sure that it had sufficient bandwidth.

To signal the importance of the long term, Ridge carried a prototype of the pen with him wherever he went. This gave Team Tomorrow the attention it needed, but it also, at least initially, exacerbated feelings among some in the marketing team that they had been left out. Ridge, Milner, and Barry all quickly saw just how important it was to celebrate the accomplishments of the core business's team as well.

Ridge took other steps that contributed to WD-40's success. He made it clear that he would evaluate all involved employees on their effectiveness in collaborating across organizational boundaries. And he was able to lessen the anxiety about cannibalization by collecting data and sharing analyses that showed that the No-Mess Pen generated purely incremental sales.

engine leaders. These negotiations are best resolved through a single plan and budgeting process for the entire innovation initiative, with conflicts directly adjudicated by the senior executive.

In other cases, the competition is for the attention of the shared staff. It's tempting for the innovation leader to think that once the budget for an initiative is approved, the fight for resources is over. It is not. Each shared staff member chooses how much energy to devote to the new initiative every day. The innovation leader's powers of persuasion are critical but may not be adequate. Some companies create special incentives and targets for shared staff members to spur them to keep up with the demands of both innovation and ongoing operations. Others charge the innovation initiative for the shared staff's time. That way, the shared staff treats the innovation leader more like a customer than a distraction.

Emotional conflicts must also be managed. Sometimes resentments are grounded in substantive business conflicts, like the possibility that the innovation initiative may cannibalize the existing business. Senior executives must argue clearly and consistently that the innovation initiative is nonetheless in the company's long-term best interest and do as much as possible to allay fears about job security.

At other times, resentments amount to simple jealousy. The performance engine may feel disenfranchised if the innovation initiative is viewed as the company's most critical project. Or the dedicated team may feel marginalized as pursuers of a quirky experiment. Some companies have countered the effects of envy by making "ability to work productively with internal partners" a key assessment in individual performance reviews.

The briefs project at West faced multiple kinds of conflict but overcame them. Steve Anderson provided the right type of leadership. He viewed the performance engine as his partner, not his enemy. And he received constant support from two senior leaders, Mike Wilens and Erv Barbre.

Wilens and Barbre paid close attention to resource conflicts. When Barbre asked members of the shared staff to make contributions to the briefs effort, he also explicitly discussed what was on their plates and what could be deferred. In some cases, he hired contract labor to help with routine tasks, such as loading documents, to ensure that the priorities of both innovation and ongoing operations could be met.

Meanwhile, Anderson recognized the importance of galvanizing the shared staff. He and his team got people on board by, among other things, creating a skit based on the *Perry Mason* television series. It showed what a lawyer's life was really like and why a product like a briefs database would be enormously valuable. Wilens and Barbre backed up his effort, in part by creating a special incentive for the sales force to push the new offering. All three leaders monitored emotional tensions. As the briefs project started to show signs of success, they saw that some in the performance engine felt as though they had been left out of a real "glamour project." The leaders countered by reinforcing the importance of the core business and by holding events at which they spread credit as widely as possible, within both the dedicated team and the performance engine.

## The Unlikeliest Partnership Is Manageable

The reception of West's briefs database exceeded expectations. In fact, the company was deluged with queries about how quickly the database would be expanded to include additional legal specialties and jurisdictions. The company followed with many more initiatives like it, such as new databases of expert testimony and court dockets.

The organizational formula was not always the same for those initiatives. For example, when West pursued a product called Peer-Monitor, it assigned almost the entire job—development and commercialization—to the dedicated team. PeerMonitor provided data that enabled law firms to benchmark their business performance against that of rivals. West chose to assign sales and marketing to the dedicated team because selling PeerMonitor required a different skill set and a longer cycle. The target customer was also different: West sold most of its offerings to law librarians, but PeerMonitor was sold directly to managing partners. The PeerMonitor sales force collaborated with the performance engine's sales force to coordinate an overall approach.

West's example is one worthy of study. The company succeeded where others have stumbled because it saw that innovation is not something that happens either inside or outside the existing organization, and that innovation does not require that an upstart fight the establishment. Instead, innovation requires a partnership between a newly formed team and the long-standing one.

While such partnerships are challenging, they are manageable. And they are indispensable. Indeed, without them, innovation goes nowhere.

**Originally published in July 2010. Reprint** R1007F

# How GE Is Disrupting Itself

*by Jeffrey R. Immelt, Vijay Govindarajan, and Chris Trimble*

IN MAY 2009, General Electric announced that over the next six years it would spend $3 billion to create at least 100 health-care innovations that would substantially lower costs, increase access, and improve quality. Two products it highlighted at the time—a $1,000 handheld electrocardiogram device and a portable, PC-based ultrasound machine that sells for as little as $15,000—are revolutionary, and not just because of their small size and low price. They're also extraordinary because they originally were developed for markets in emerging economies (the ECG device for rural India and the ultrasound machine for rural China) and are now being sold in the United States, where they're pioneering new uses for such machines.

We call the process used to develop the two machines and take them global *reverse innovation,* because it's the opposite of the *glocalization* approach that many industrial-goods manufacturers based in rich countries have employed for decades. With glocalization, companies develop great products at home and then distribute them worldwide, with some adaptations to local conditions. It allows multinationals to make the optimal trade-off between the global scale so crucial to minimizing costs and the local customization required to maximize market share. Glocalization worked fine in an era when rich countries accounted for the vast majority of the market and other countries didn't offer much opportunity. But those days are over—thanks to the rapid development of populous countries like China and India and the slowing growth of wealthy nations.

GE badly needs innovations like the low-cost ECG and ultrasound machines, not only to expand beyond high-end segments in places like China and India but also to preempt local companies in those countries—the emerging giants—from creating similar products and then using them to disrupt GE in rich countries. To put it bluntly: If GE's businesses are to survive and prosper in the next decade, they must become as adept at reverse innovation as they are at glocalization. Success in developing countries is a prerequisite for continued vitality in developed ones.

The problem is that there are deep conflicts between glocalization and reverse innovation. And the company can't simply replace the first with the second, because glocalization will continue to dominate strategy for the foreseeable future. The two models need to do more than coexist; they need to cooperate. This is a heck of a lot easier said than done since the centralized, product-focused structures and practices that have made multinationals so successful at glocalization actually get in the way of reverse innovation, which requires a decentralized, local-market focus.

Almost all the people and resources dedicated to reverse innovation efforts must be based and managed in the local market. These local growth teams need to have P&L responsibility; the power to decide which products to develop for their markets and how to make, sell, and service them; and the right to draw from the company's global resources. Once products have proven themselves in emerging markets, they must be taken global, which may involve pioneering radically new applications, establishing lower price points, and even using the innovations to cannibalize higher-margin products in rich countries. All of those approaches are antithetical to the glocalization model. This article aims to share what GE has learned in trying to overcome that conflict.

# Idea in Brief

For decades, General Electric and other industrial-goods manufacturers based in rich countries grew by developing high-end products at home and distributing them globally, with some adaptations to local conditions—an approach known as glocalization. Now they must do an about-face and learn to bring low-end products created specifically for emerging markets into wealthy markets. That process, called reverse innovation, isn't easy to master. It requires a decentralized, local-market focus that clashes with the centralized, product-focused structure that multinationals have evolved for glocalization. In this article, Immelt, GE's CEO, and Govindarajan and Trimble, of Dartmouth's Tuck School of Business, describe how GE has dealt with that challenge. An anomaly within the ultrasound unit of GE Healthcare provided the blueprint. Because China's poorly funded rural clinics couldn't afford the company's sophisticated ultrasound machines, a local team built a cheap, portable ultrasound out of a laptop equipped with special peripherals and software. It not only became a hit in China but jump-started growth in the developed world by pioneering applications for situations where portability is critical, such as at accident sites. The team succeeded because a top executive championed it and gave it unprecedented autonomy. GE has since set up more than a dozen similar operations in an effort to expand beyond the premium segments in developing countries—and to preempt emerging giants from disrupting GE's sales at home

## Why Reverse Innovation Is So Important

Glocalization is so dominant today because it has delivered. Largely because of glocalization, GE's revenues outside the United States soared from $4.8 billion, or 19% of total revenues, in 1980, to $97 billion, or more than half of the total, in 2008.

The model came to prominence when opportunities in today's emerging markets were pretty limited—when their economies had yet to take off and their middle or low-end customer segments didn't exist. Therefore, it made sense for multinational manufacturers to simply offer them modifications of products for developed countries. Initially, GE, like other multinationals, was satisfied with the 15% to 20% growth rates its businesses enjoyed in developing countries, thanks to glocalization.

Then in September 2001 one of the coauthors of this piece, Jeff Immelt, who had just become GE's CEO, set a goal: to greatly accelerate organic growth at the company and become less dependent on acquisitions. This made people question many things that had been taken for granted, including the glocalization strategy, which limited the company to skimming the top of emerging markets. A rigorous analysis of GE's health-care, power-generation, and power-distribution businesses showed that if they took full advantage of opportunities that glocalization had ignored in heavily populated places like China and India, they could grow two to three times faster there. But to do that, they'd have to develop innovative new products that met the specific needs and budgets of customers in those markets. That realization, in turn, led GE executives to question two core tenets of glocalization.

### Assumption 1: Emerging economies will largely evolve in the same way that wealthy economies did

The reality is, developing countries aren't following the same path and could actually jump ahead of developed countries because of their greater willingness to adopt breakthrough innovations. With far smaller per capita incomes, developing countries are more than happy with high-tech solutions that deliver decent performance at an ultralow cost—a 50% solution at a 15% price. And they lack many of the legacy infrastructures of the developed world, which were built when conditions were very different. They need communications, energy, and transportation products that address today's challenges and opportunities, such as unpredictable oil prices and ubiquitous wireless technologies. Finally, because of their huge populations, sustainability problems are especially urgent for countries like China and India. Because of this, they're likely to tackle many environmental issues years or even decades before the developed world.

All this isn't theory. It's already happening. Emerging markets are becoming centers of innovation in fields like low-cost health-care devices, carbon sequestration, solar and wind power, biofuels, distributed power generation, batteries, water desalination, micro-finance, electric cars, and even ultra-low-cost homes.

### Assumption 2: Products that address developing countries' special needs can't be sold in developed countries because they're not good enough to compete there

The reality here is, these products can create brand-new markets in the developed world—by establishing dramatically lower price points or pioneering new applications.

Consider GE's health-care business in the United States. It used to make most of its money on premium computed tomography (CT) and magnetic resonance (MR) imaging machines. But to succeed in the era of broader access and reduced reimbursement that President Obama hopes to bring about, the business will probably need to increase by 50% the number of products it offers at lower price points. And that doesn't mean just cheaper versions of high-tech products like imaging machines. The company also must create more offerings like the heated bassinet it developed for India, which has great potential in U.S. inner cities, where infant deaths related to the cold remain high.

And let's not forget that technology often can be improved until it satisfies more demanding customers. The compact ultrasound, which can now handle imaging applications that previously required a conventional machine, is one example. (See the exhibit "Reverse innovation in practice.") Another is an aircraft engine that GE acquired when it bought a Czech aerospace company for $20 million. GE invested an additional $25 million to further develop the engine's technology and now plans to use it to challenge Pratt & Whitney's dominance of the small turboprop market in developed countries. GE's cost position is probably half of what Pratt's is.

## Preempting the Emerging Giants

Before the financial crisis plunged the world into a deep recession, GE's leaders had been looking to emerging markets to help achieve their ambitious growth objectives. Now they're counting on these

# Reverse innovation in practice

## 1 Original product

**Conventional ultrasound 2002 price**

**$100K and up**

In the 1990s GE served the Chinese ultrasound market with machines developed in the U.S. and Japan.

Typical customers

- Sophisticated hospital imaging centers

Typical uses

- Cardiology (such as measuring the size of passages or blood flow in the heart)
- Obstetrics (monitoring fetal health)
- General radiology (assessing prostate health, for example)

But the expensive, bulky devices sold poorly in China.

## 2 The emerging market disruption

**Portable ultrasound 2002 price**

**$30K–$40K**

**2007 price**

**$15K**

In 2002 a local team in China leveraged GE's global resources to develop a cheap, portable machine using a laptop computer enhanced with a probe and sophisticated software.

In 2007 the team launched a dramatically cheaper model. Sales in China took off.

Typical customers

- China: rural clinics
- U.S.: ambulance squads and emergency rooms

Typical uses

- China: spotting enlarged livers and gallbladder stones
- U.S.: in emergency rooms to identify ectopic pregnancies; at accident sites to check for fluid around the heart; in operating rooms to place catheters for anesthesia

## 3 The new global market

**Portable ultrasound global revenues**

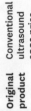

$4M 2002

2008 $278M

**Portable ultrasound 2009 price**

**$15K–$100K**

**Conventional ultrasound 2009 price**

**$100K–$350K**

Thanks to technology advances, higher-priced PC-based models can now perform radiology and obstetrics functions that once required a conventional machine.

markets even more because they think that after the downturn ends, the developed world will suffer a prolonged period of slow growth—1% to 3% a year. In contrast, annual growth in emerging markets could easily reach two to three times that rate.

Ten years ago when GE senior managers discussed the global marketplace, they talked about "the U.S., Europe, Japan, and the rest of the world." Now they talk about "resource-rich regions," such as the Middle East, Brazil, Canada, Australia, and Russia, and "people-rich regions," such as China and India. The "rest of world" means the U.S., Europe, and Japan.

To be honest, the company also is embracing reverse innovation for defensive reasons. If GE doesn't come up with innovations in poor countries and take them global, new competitors from the developing world—like Mindray, Suzlon, Goldwind, and Haier—will.

In GE's markets the Chinese will be bigger players than the Indians will. The Chinese have a real plan to become a major global force in transportation and power generation. GE Power Generation is already regularly running into Chinese enterprises as it competes in Africa, which will be an extremely important region for the company. One day those enterprises may compete with GE in its own backyard.

That's a bracing prospect. GE has tremendous respect for traditional rivals like Siemens, Philips, and Rolls-Royce. But it knows how to compete with them; they will never destroy GE. By introducing products that create a new price-performance paradigm, however, the emerging giants very well could. Reverse innovation isn't optional; it's oxygen.

## A Clash of Two Models

Glocalization has defined international strategy for three decades. All the currently dominant ideas—from Christopher A. Bartlett and Sumantra Ghoshal's "transnational" strategy to Pankaj Ghemawat's "adaptation-aggregation" trade-off—fit within the glocalization framework. Since organization follows strategy, it's hardly surprising that glocalization also has molded the way that multinationals are structured and run.

GE is a case in point. For the past 30 years, its organization has evolved to maximize its effectiveness at glocalization. Power and P&L responsibility were concentrated in global business units headquartered in the developed world. The major business functions—including R&D, manufacturing, and marketing—were centralized at headquarters. While some R&D centers and manufacturing operations were moved abroad to tap overseas talent and reduce costs, they focused mainly on products for wealthy countries.

While this approach has enormous advantages, it makes reverse innovation impossible. The experiences of Venkatraman Raja, the head of GE Healthcare's business in India, illustrate why.

GE Healthcare sells an x-ray imaging product called a surgical C-arm, which is used in basic surgeries. A high-quality, high-priced product designed for hospitals in wealthy countries, it has proven tough to sell in India. Raja saw the problem and made a proposal in 2005. He wanted to develop, manufacture, and sell a simpler, easier-to-use, and substantially cheaper product in India. His proposal made sense, and yet, to no one's surprise, it was not approved.

If you were a leader of a GE operation in a developing country, as Raja was, here's what you were up against: Your formal responsibilities included neither general management nor product development. Your responsibility was to sell, distribute, and service GE's global products locally and provide insights into customers' needs to help the company adapt its offerings. You were expected to grow revenues by 15% to 20% a year and make sure that costs increased at a much slower rate, so that margins rose. You were held rigidly accountable for delivering on plan. Just finding the time for an extracurricular activity like creating a proposal for a product tailored to the local market was challenging.

That was nothing, however, compared with the challenge of the next step: selling your proposal internally. Doing so required getting the attention of the general manager at headquarters in the United States, who sat two or more levels above your immediate boss and was far more familiar with a world-renowned medical center in

Boston than a rural clinic outside Bangalore. Even if you got the meeting, you'd have limited time to make your case. (India accounted for just 1% of GE's revenues at the time and occupied roughly the same mindshare of managers with global responsibility.)

If you were extremely persuasive, you might be invited to share the proposal with others. But when you visited the head of global manufacturing, you'd have to counter arguments that a simple, streamlined global product line was much more efficient than custom offerings. When you visited the head of marketing, you'd have to deal with fears that a lower-priced product would weaken the GE brand and cannibalize existing sales. When you met with the head of finance, you'd have to wrestle with concerns that lower-priced products would drag down overall margins. And when you visited the head of global R&D, you'd have to explain why the energies of GE's scientists and engineers—including those in technology centers in emerging markets—should be diverted from projects directed at its most sophisticated customers, who paid top dollar.

Even if you gained support from each of these executives and got the proposal off the ground, you'd still have to compete for capital year after year against more certain projects with shorter-term payoffs. Meanwhile, of course, you'd still have to worry about making your quarterly numbers for your day job.

It was little wonder that successful efforts to develop radically new products for poor countries were extremely rare.

## Shifting the Center of Gravity

Obviously, changing long-established structures, practices, and attitudes is an enormous task. As is the case in any major change program, the company's top leaders have to play a major role.

To do so, they must investigate firsthand the size of the opportunity and how it could be exploited and encourage the teams running the corporation's businesses to do the same. As GE's CEO, Jeff goes to China and India two times a year. When he's in, say, China, he'll spend a day at GE's research center in Shanghai and then meet separately with dozens of people in the company's local business operations and just let them talk about what they're working on, what their cost points are, who their competitors are, and so on. On such visits, he has realized that there's a whole realm of technology that the company should be applying faster.

While in China, Jeff will also talk with government leaders, including Premier Wen Jiabao. Wen has told Jeff about his plans to develop China's economy and how making health care affordable for all citizens fits into that. It takes a conversation like that to fully appreciate the opportunities in China.

In India, Jeff will have dinner with the CEOs of Indian companies. At one dinner Anand Mahindra talked about how his company, Mahindra & Mahindra, was making life miserable for John Deere in India with a tractor that cost half the price of Deere's but was still enormously profitable. Such discussions drive home the point that you can make a lot of money in India if you have the right business models.

So the job of the CEO—of any senior business leader, for that matter—is to connect all the dots and then act as a catalyst. It's to give initiatives special status and funding and personally monitor them on a monthly or quarterly basis. And perhaps most important in the case of reverse innovation, it's to push your enterprise to come up with the new organizational form that will allow product and business-model innovation to flourish in emerging markets.

## A Homegrown Model

To develop that new organizational form, GE did what it has always done: learn from other companies' experiences but also try to find an internal group that somehow had managed to overcome the hurdles and achieve success. During their annual strategy review, the company's leaders spotted one in the ultrasound unit of GE Healthcare.

GE Healthcare's primary business is high-end medical-imaging equipment. By the late 1980s it had become clear that a new technology—ultrasound—had a bright future. Ultrasound machines, like the other imaging devices, were typically found in sophisticated imaging centers in hospitals. While they delivered lower quality than CT or MR scanners, they did so at much lower cost. The company aimed to be number one in ultrasound.

Over the next decade, GE Healthcare expanded its presence in the market. It built an R&D facility for developing new ultrasound products near its headquarters, in Milwaukee, and made acquisitions and entered into joint ventures around the world. It competed in all three of the primary market segments—obstetrics, cardiology, and general radiology—by launching premium products that employed cutting-edge technologies. By 2000, GE Healthcare had established solid market positions in rich countries around the world.

The results in developing countries, by contrast, were disappointing. By 2000, with the help of a joint venture partner in China, GE saw the problem: In wealthy countries performance mattered most, followed by features; in China price mattered most, followed by portability and ease of use.

The priorities weren't the same because the health-care infrastructure of China was so different from that of rich countries. More than 90% of China's population relied (and still relies) on poorly funded, low-tech hospitals or basic clinics in rural villages. These facilities had no sophisticated imaging centers, and transportation to urban hospitals was difficult, especially for the sick. Patients couldn't come to the ultrasound machines; the ultrasound machines, therefore, had to go to the patients.

There was no way that GE could meet that need by simply scaling down, removing features from, or otherwise adapting its existing ultrasound machines, which were large, bulky, expensive, and complex. It needed a revolutionary product.

In 2002, the company launched its first compact ultrasound, which combined a regular laptop computer with sophisticated software. It sold for as low as $30,000. In late 2007, GE introduced a model that sold for as low as $15,000, less than 15% of the cost of GE's high-end ultrasound machines. Of course, its performance was not as high, but it was nonetheless a hit in rural clinics, where doctors used it for simple applications, such as spotting enlarged livers and gallbladders and stomach irregularities. The software-centric design also made it easy to adjust the machine—for example, to improve the interfaces—after observing how doctors worked with it. Today the portable machine is the growth engine of GE's ultrasound business in China.

Even more exciting, the innovation has generated dramatic growth in the developed world by pioneering new applications where portability is critical or space is constrained, such as at accident sites, where the compacts are used to diagnose problems like pericardial effusions (fluid around the heart); in emergency rooms, where they are employed to identify conditions such as ectopic pregnancies; and in operating rooms, where they aid anesthesiologists in placing needles and catheters.

Six years after their launch, portable ultrasounds were a $278 million global product line for GE, one that was growing at 50% to 60% a year before the worldwide recession hit. Someday every general practitioner may carry both a stethoscope and a compact ultrasound device embedded in his or her PDA.

The products owe their successful development to an organizational anomaly in GE: the existence of multiple ultrasound business units. Although the three primary segments of the ultrasound business are vastly different, GE's initial instinct was to follow the glocalization model when it built the business—that is, to create a single integrated global organization. In 1995, however, Omar Ishrak, a newcomer who had been hired to lead the business, saw that meshing operations would reduce them to a common denominator that served nobody well. He decided to run the business as three independent business units with their own P&L responsibility, all reporting to him.

When the compact ultrasound effort began in China, Ishrak saw that the new business would have little in common with the three units, which were focused on premium products. So instead, he created a fourth independent unit, based in Wuxi, China. It evolved the local growth team (LGT) model, which is based on five critical principles.

## 1. Shift power to where the growth is
Without autonomy, the LGTs will become pawns of the global business and won't be able to focus on the problems of customers in emerging markets. Specifically, they need the power to develop

their own strategies, organizations, and products. Ishrak understood this and gave such broad authority to Diana Tang and J.K. Koo, the leaders of GE's ultrasound effort in China. The pair of GE veterans had deep experience in the ultrasound business, expertise in biomedical engineering and general management, and lengthy careers in Asia.

## 2. Build new offerings from the ground up

Given the tremendous gulfs between rich countries and poor ones in income, infrastructure, and sustainability needs, reverse innovation must be zero-based. These wide differences cannot be spanned by adapting global products.

The compact ultrasound was built from scratch, although it drew heavily from an existing R&D effort. In the late 1990s, in a product-development center in Israel, GE had started to experiment with a revolutionary new architecture—one that shifted most of the muscle inside an ultrasound machine from the hardware to the software. Instead of a large box full of custom hardware, the scientists and engineers involved in the project envisioned a standard high-performance PC, special peripherals such as an ultrasound probe, and sophisticated software.

The concept generated little excitement in GE Healthcare at the time because it could not come close to matching the performance of the business's premium products. But Ishrak quickly saw the value of the new architecture in developing countries. He encouraged the team in China to pursue the concept further. The resulting compact ultrasound based on a laptop computer hit the mark in China.

## 3. Build LGTs from the ground up, like new companies

Zero-based innovation doesn't happen without zero-based organizational design. GE's organizational "software"—its hiring practices, reporting structures, titles, job descriptions, norms for working relationships, and power balances between functions—all evolved to support glocalization. LGTs need to rewrite the software.

Tang and Koo constructed a business unit that managed a complete value chain: product development, sourcing, manufacturing, marketing, sales, and service. By recruiting locally, they were able to find most of the expertise they needed—including engineers with deep knowledge of miniaturization and low-power consumption and a commercialization team well versed in health care in rural China.

The LGT also decided that dealers—rather than the direct sales force used by the premium ultrasound units—were the only cost-effective way to reach China's vast and fragmented rural markets and third-tier cities. And instead of relying on GE Healthcare's global customer-support and replacement-parts organizations, it built in-country teams that could provide quicker and less costly service.

## 4. Customize objectives, targets, and metrics

Innovation endeavors are, by nature, uncertain. It's more important to learn quickly by efficiently testing assumptions than to hit the numbers. So the relevant metrics and standards for LGTs—the ones that resolve the critical unknowns—are rarely the same as those used by the established businesses.

The ultrasound LGT knew that doctors in rural China were less familiar with ultrasounds than doctors in cities. But the team didn't know how much experience rural doctors had with the technology or what features would meet their needs. So it set out to learn how doctors reacted to the machines and what the obstacles to their adoption were. The team discovered that ease of use, especially in primary-care screenings, where doctors test for common local conditions, was even more crucial than anticipated. In response, the new business emphasized training, offered online guides, designed simpler keyboards, created built-in presets for certain tasks, and tracked customer satisfaction to gauge success.

Ishrak was careful to use different criteria to evaluate the performance of the LGT in China. For example, because the government approval process for new product releases is less intricate in China, he set much shorter product-development cycles than were common in wealthy countries. He also agreed to allow the size of the local service organization to deviate from the GE Healthcare's global standards. Since salaries are lower and service is more demanding in

China, a bigger staff relative to the number of installed machines made sense.

## 5. Have the LGT report to someone high in the organization

LGTs cannot thrive without strong support from the top. The executive overseeing the LGT has three critical roles: mediating conflicts between the team and the global business, connecting the team to resources such as global R&D centers, and helping take the innovations that the team develops into rich countries. Only a senior executive in the global business unit, or even its leader, can accomplish all of that.

Even when it was tiny, the LGT in China reported directly to Ishrak. Because GE Healthcare had an ambitious product-development agenda for rich countries when the compact project was launched, the LGT's engineers might easily have been redirected to other projects if Ishrak hadn't shielded the team. He protected and even expanded the team's resources. By 2007 its number of engineers had grown from 13 to 70 and its total payroll had increased from 132 to 339. Ishrak also personally made sure that the team got the expertise it needed from other parts of GE, such as three highly respected development engineers from Israel, Japan, and South Korea. They worked full-time on the project and got it extra support from GE's R&D centers around the world.

Ishrak included the China LGT in the company's Ultrasound Council, a group of ultrasound executives and market and technology experts who meet for two days three times a year. At the meeting they share knowledge and insights and agree on which major projects to pursue. The council was instrumental in moving knowledge and technology into China.

Finally, Ishrak played a critical role in building a global market for the portable ultrasound. He identified potential new applications in the developed world and saw to it that the three units that sold the premium products aggressively pursued those opportunities.

---

GE now has more than a dozen local growth teams in China and India. In the midst of a severe global recession, GE's businesses in

China will grow 25% this year—largely because of LGTs. It's way too early to declare victory, however. Progress has been uneven. While some businesses—notably, health care and power generation and distribution—have taken the ball and run with it, others have been less enthusiastic. And though GE's R&D centers in China and India have increased their focus on the problems of developing countries, the vast majority of their resources are still devoted to initiatives for developed ones. So there is still a long way to go.

It's still necessary for the company's top executives to monitor and protect local efforts and make sure they get resources. It's still necessary to experiment with people transfers, organizational structures, and processes to see what works. The biggest experiment is about to come: To speed progress in India, GE is creating a separate P&L that will include all GE businesses in that country and giving the new unit considerable power to tap GE's global R&D resources. It will be headed by a senior vice president who will report to a vice chairman. That's anathema in a company used to a matrix in which product comes first and country second. Nonetheless, the company is going to try it and see if it can create new markets. GE has to learn how to operate on a different axis.

The resistance to giving India its own P&L reflects what is perhaps GE's biggest challenge: changing the mind-set of managers who've spent their careers excelling at glocalization. Even the exemplars have a rich-country bias. In a recent conversation with Jeff, one such manager—the head of a major business that's doing well in India and China—still seemed preoccupied with problems beyond his control in the U.S. "I don't even want to talk to you about your growth plans for the U.S.," Jeff responded. "You've got to triple the size of your Indian business in the next three years. You've got to put more resources, more people, and more products in there, so you're deep in that market and not just skimming the very top. Let's figure out how to do it." That's how senior managers have to think.

**Originally published in October 2009. Reprint R0910D**

# The Customer-Centered Innovation Map

*by Lance A. Bettencourt and Anthony W. Ulwick*

**WE ALL KNOW THAT** people "hire" products and services to get a job done. Office workers hire word-processing software to create documents and digital recorders to capture meeting notes. Surgeons hire scalpels to dissect soft tissue and electrocautery devices to control patient bleeding. Janitors hire soap dispensers, paper towels, and cleansing fluid to help remove grime from their hands.

While all this seems obvious, very few companies use the perspective of "getting the job done" to discover opportunities for innovation. In fact, the innovation journey for many companies is little more than hopeful wandering through customer interviews. Such unsystematic inquiry may occasionally turn up interesting tidbits of information, but it rarely uncovers the best ideas or an exhaustive set of opportunities for growth.

We have developed an efficient yet simple system companies can use to find new ways to innovate. Our method, which we call "job mapping," breaks down the task the customer wants done into a series of discrete process steps. By deconstructing a job from beginning to end, a company gains a complete view of all the points at which a customer might desire more help from a product or service—namely, at each step in the job. With a job map in hand, a company can analyze the biggest drawbacks of the products and services customers currently use. Job mapping also gives companies a comprehensive framework with which to identify the metrics customers themselves use to measure success in executing a task. (For a description of these metrics and a discussion about how to gather and prioritize them, see Anthony W. Ulwick's "Turn Customer Input into Innovation" in HBR's January 2002 issue.)

Job mapping differs substantively from process mapping in that the goal is to identify what customers are *trying* to get done at every step, not what they are doing currently. For example, when an anesthesiologist checks a monitor during a surgical procedure, the action taken is just a means to an end. Detecting a change in patient vital signs is the job the anesthesiologist is trying to get done. By mapping out every step of the job and locating opportunities for innovative solutions, companies can discover new ways to differentiate their offerings.

## Anatomy of a Customer Job

Over the past 10 years, we have mapped customer jobs in dozens of product and service categories that span professional and consumer services, durable and consumable goods, chemicals, software, and many other industries. Our work has revealed three fundamental principles about customer jobs.

### All jobs are processes

Every job, from transplanting a heart to cleaning a floor, has a distinct beginning, middle, and end, and comprises a set of process steps along the way. The starting point for identifying innovation opportunities is to map out—from the customer's perspective—the steps involved in executing a particular job. Once the steps are identified, a company can create value in a number of ways—by improving the execution of specific job steps; eliminating the need for particular inputs or outputs; removing an entire step from the responsibility of the customer; addressing an overlooked step;

## Idea in Brief

We all know that people "hire" products to get jobs done. Office workers hire word-processing software to create documents. Surgeons hire scalpels to dissect soft tissue. But few companies keep this in mind while searching for ideas for breakthrough offerings. Instead, they rely on inquiry methods (such as customer interviews) that don't generate the most promising ideas or exhaustive sets of possibilities.

To systematically uncover more—and better—innovative ideas, Bettencourt and Ulwick recommend

**job mapping:** Break down a job that customers want done into discrete steps. Then brainstorm ways to make steps easier, faster, or unnecessary.

For example, while cleaning clothes, people don't notice stubborn stains until they've taken the clothes from a dryer and started folding them. If they find a stain, they must repeat the job. A washer that detects persistent stains and takes appropriate action *before* consumers execute the rest of the job would have huge appeal.

resequencing the steps; or enabling steps to be completed in new locations or at different times.

When mapping the job of washing clothes, for example, a company would quickly discover that the step of "verifying that stains have been removed" often comes at the end of the job sequence, after the clothes have been removed from the washing machine, dried, folded, and put away—too late to do much of anything about it. If the washing machine itself could detect the presence of any remaining stains before the wash cycle ended—resequence when verification takes place—it could take the necessary actions at a much more convenient point in the job. If the machine could be designed to remove the need for inputs such as stain removers and bleach, that would be even better.

### All jobs have a universal structure

That universal structure, regardless of the customer, has the following process steps: defining what the job requires; identifying and locating needed inputs; preparing the components and the physical environment; confirming that everything is ready; executing the task;

# Idea in Practice

All jobs have the same eight steps. To use job mapping, look for opportunities to help customers at every step:

| During this step . . . | Customers . . . | Companies can innovate by . . . | Example |
|---|---|---|---|
| 1: Define | Determine their goals and plan resources. | Simplifying planning. | Weight Watchers streamlines diet planning by offering a system that doesn't require calorie counting. |
| 2: Locate | Gather items and information needed to do the job. | Making required inputs easier to gather and ensuring they're available when and where needed. | U-Haul provides customers with prepackaged moving kits containing the number and types of boxes required for a move. |
| 3: Prepare | Set up the environment to do the job. | Making set-up less difficult and creating guides to ensure proper set-up of the work area. | Bosch added adjustable levers to its circular saw to accommodate common bevel angles used by roofers to cut wood. |
| 4: Confirm | Verify that they're ready to perform the job. | Giving customers information they need to confirm readiness. | Oracle's ProfitLogic merchandising optimization software confirms optimal timing and level of a store's markdowns for each product. |
| 5: Execute | Carry out the job. | Preventing problems or delays. | Kimberly-Clark's Patient Warning System automatically circulates heated water through thermal pads placed on surgery patients to maintain their normal body temperature during surgery. |

| During this step . . . | Customers . . . | Companies can innovate by . . . | Example |
|---|---|---|---|
| **6: Monitor** | Assess whether the job is being successfully executed. | Linking monitoring with improved execution. | Nike makes a running shoe containing a sensor that communicates audio feedback about time, distance, pace, and calories burned to an iPod worn by the runner. |
| **7: Modify** | Make alterations to improve execution. | Reducing the need to make alterations and the number of alterations needed. | By automatically downloading and installing updates, Microsoft's operating systems remove hassles for computer users. People don't have to determine which updates are necessary, find the updates, or ensure the updates are compatible with their operating system. |
| **8: Conclude** | Finish the job or prepare to repeat it. | Designing products that simplify the process of concluding the job. | 3M makes a wound dressing that stretches and adheres only to itself—not to patients' skin or sutures. It thus offers a convenient way for medical personnel to secure dressings at the conclusion of treatment and then remove them after a wound has healed. |

monitoring the results and the environment; making modifications; and concluding the job. Because problems can occur at many points in the process, nearly all jobs also require a problem resolution step.

Some steps are more critical than others, depending on the job, but each is necessary to get the job done successfully. For example, when preparing for the task of replacing a hip joint, surgeons sterilize their hands, establish a sterile field between their body and the patient, prep the patient's skin for the incision, and properly position the patient. A janitor about to clean his hands might prepare by simply rolling up his sleeves. Innovation possibilities reside within each of the job steps.

### Jobs are separate from solutions

Customers hire different products or services to get the same job done. When preparing income taxes, for example, one person might rely on the services of a CPA, whereas another might use tax preparation software. Others might hire both for different steps in the process.

Many companies are focused on the product or service they're already developing, or on the one the competition is offering, rather than on the help they must give the customer to execute the steps in a job. When the job is the focal point of value creation, companies not only can improve their existing offerings but also can target new, or "blue ocean," market space. While other MP3 manufacturers were concentrating on helping customers listen to music, for example, Apple reconsidered the entire job of music management, enabling customers to acquire, organize, listen to, and share music.

Taken together, these fundamental principles form the foundation of a company's search for opportunities to create customer value.

## Creating a Job Map

The goal of creating a job map is not to find out how the customer is executing a job—that only generates maps of existing activities and solutions. Instead the aim is to discover what the customer is trying to get done at different points in executing a job and what must happen at each juncture in order for the job to be carried out successfully. (See the sidebar "Mapping a Customer Job.") Let's look at the steps in detail.

## 1: Define

What aspects of getting the job done must the customer define up front in order to proceed? This step includes determining objectives; planning the approach; assessing which resources are necessary or available to complete the job; and selecting resources. A financial adviser may label this step "assessing the investment situation," since she must not only gauge investment priorities and risk tolerance but also consider how much money is available and which types of investments to select. An anesthesiologist might call it "formulating the anesthesia plan," since he must choose which type of anesthesia to provide, depending upon case characteristics and the patient's medical history.

In this step, a company can look for ways to help customers understand their objectives, simplify the resource-planning process, and reduce the amount of planning needed. Consider how Weight Watchers assists dieters with the daunting task of losing weight. The company offers a core weight-loss plan that helps the dieter select appropriate foods without the need to count calories, carbohydrates, or anything else. In addition, it provides meal ideas and recipes that fit into its core and points-based diet plans. For dieters desiring more flexibility, Weight Watchers offers instant access to point values for over 27,000 foods and online tools to help dieters gauge the impact of what they eat.

## 2: Locate

What inputs or items must the customer locate to do the job? Inputs are both tangible (for example, the surgical tools a nurse must locate for an operation) and intangible (say, business or other requirements that a software developer uses when writing code). When tangible

# Mapping a Customer Job

**TO FIND WAYS TO INNOVATE,** deconstruct the job a customer is trying to get done. By working through the questions here, you can map a customer job in just a handful of interviews with customers and internal experts.

Start by understanding the execution step, to establish context and a frame of reference. Next, examine each step before execution and then after, to uncover the role each plays in getting the job done.

To ensure that you are mapping job steps (what the customer is trying to accomplish) rather than process solutions (what is currently being done), ask yourself the validating questions below at each step.

### Validating Questions

As defined, does the step specify what the customer is trying to accomplish, or is it only being done to accomplish a more fundamental goal?

> **Valid step:** ascertain patient vital signs
>
> **Invalid step:** check the monitor

Does the step apply universally for any customer executing the job, or does it depend on how a particular customer does the job?

> **Valid step:** place an order
>
> **Invalid step:** call the supplier to place an order

### Defining the Execution Step

What are the most central tasks that must be accomplished in getting the job done?

- **Validate the steps**

---

materials are involved, a company might consider streamlining this step by making the required components easier to gather, ensuring that they are available when and where needed, or eliminating the need for some inputs altogether. Consider how U-Haul helps customers locate the inputs necessary to complete the job of moving their physical goods. In addition to being a one-stop shop for moving supplies, U-Haul offers customers prepackaged moving kits that

### Defining Pre-Execution Steps

What must happen before the core execution step to ensure the job is successfully carried out?

- What must be defined or planned before the execution step?

- What must be located or gathered?

- What must be prepared or set up?

- What must be confirmed before the execution step?

- **Validate the steps**

### Defining Post-Execution Steps

What must happen after the core execution step to ensure the job is successfully carried out?

- What must be monitored or verified after the execution step to ensure the job is successfully performed?

- What must be modified or adjusted after the execution step?

- What must be done to properly conclude the job or to prepare for the next job cycle?

- **Validate the steps**

reduce the time it takes to gather the various boxes and supplies required for a move. In addition, an online partnership with eMove helps customers quickly locate a variety of inputs in the form of human helpers—packers, babysitters, cleaners, and painters. Opportunities abound to help customers assemble intangible materials as well: for instance, retrieve stored data, facilitate the collection of new information, and verify that data are accurate and complete.

## 3: Prepare

How must the customer prepare the inputs and environment to do the job? Nearly all customer jobs involve an element of setting up and organizing materials. Before cooking french fries, the fast-food operator must open bags, portion, and load fries into baskets; the nurse must set out and organize surgical tools before an operation can begin. It may also be necessary to prepare a working surface or some other aspect of the physical environment. The dentist readies the surface of a molar prior to restoring the tooth; the painter cleans the wall before applying the first coat of paint.

At this stage, companies should consider ways to make setup less difficult. They might invent a means to automate the preparation process; make it easier to organize physical materials; or create guides and safeguards to ensure the proper arrangement of the work area. (For customers dealing with information, companies can help organize, integrate, and examine required data.) Bosch learned of one opportunity to help customers prepare to cut wood when professional roofers told the company that they would like a way to speed the process of setting bevel levels on their saws. Accordingly, Bosch added adjustable levers to its CS20 circular saw to accommodate the most common bevel adjustments such as 30°, 45°, and 60°. This reduced the time needed to cut the wood and increased the accuracy of the adjustments.

## 4: Confirm

Once preparation is complete, what does the customer need to verify before proceeding with the job to ensure its successful execution? Here, the customer makes sure that materials and the working environment have been properly prepared; validates the quality and functional capacity of material and informational components; and confirms priorities when deciding among execution options. This step is especially critical for jobs in which a delay in execution might risk a customer's money, time, or safety. For example, after preparing a patient for an operation, the surgical nurse must confirm the

# Uncovering Opportunities for Innovation

**WITH A JOB MAP IN HAND,** you can begin to look systematically for opportunities to create value. The questions below can guide you in your search and help you avoid overlooking any possibilities. A great way to begin is to consider the biggest drawbacks of current solutions at each step in the map—in particular, drawbacks related to speed of execution, variability, and the quality of output. To increase the effectiveness of this approach, invite a diverse team of experts—marketing, design, engineering, and even some lead customers—to participate in this discussion.

## Opportunities at the job level

- Can the job be executed in a more efficient or effective sequence?

- Do some customers struggle more with executing the job than others (for instance, novices versus experts, older versus younger)?

- What struggles or inconveniences do customers experience because they must rely on multiple solutions to get the job done?

- Is it possible to eliminate the need for particular inputs or outputs from the job?

- Is it necessary that the customers execute all steps for which they are currently responsible? Can the burden be automated or shifted to someone else?

- How may trends affect the way the job is executed in the future?

- In what contexts do customers most struggle with executing the job today? Where else or when else might customers want to execute the job?

## Opportunities at the step level

- What causes variability (or unreliability) in executing this step? What causes execution to go off track?

- Do some customers struggle more than others with this step?

- What does this step's ideal output look like (and in what ways is the current output less than ideal)?

- Is this step more difficult to execute successfully in some contexts than others?

- What are the biggest drawbacks of current solutions used to execute this step?

- What makes executing this step time-consuming or inconvenient?

readiness of the patient (jewelry removed, vitals in check); of the equipment and instrumentation (battery power sufficient, scalpels available); and of the operating room (materials in place, sterile field intact).

A company seeking to differentiate itself at this step could help customers gain access to the types of information and feedback they need to confirm readiness and decide among execution alternatives. Another approach is to search for ways to build confirmation into the locating and preparing steps, since this would allow the customer to proceed through the job more quickly and easily. For example, Oracle's ProfitLogic merchandising optimization software removes the responsibility from the merchandiser for confirming the optimal timing and level of markdowns by analyzing thousands of different demand scenarios at the individual product level and recommending the scenario for each product that is likely to yield the highest profit.

## 5: Execute

What must customers do to execute the job successfully? Whether they're printing a document or administering anesthesia, customers consider the execution step the most important part of the job. Because execution is also the most visible step, customers are especially concerned about avoiding problems and delays, as well as achieving optimal results. An office worker who prints out a document wants to avoid paper jams, running out of toner, and long print queues. She also wants to improve the quality of printed output. An anesthesiologist wants to prevent negative patient reactions and to ensure that the patient is unable to feel pain.

Here, innovating companies can apply their technological know-how to provide customers with real-time feedback or to automatically correct execution problems. Companies can also think about ways to keep performance consistent in different contexts. Kimberly-Clark's Patient Warming System is a good example of value added in this way. The system relies on a control unit that automatically circulates heated water through thermal pads placed on the patient to avoid temperature spikes during surgery. The system can maintain normal patient temperature with only 20% of the patient body covered, which means the device performs consistently and efficiently in a variety of complex surgical procedures.

## 6: Monitor

What does the customer need to monitor to ensure that the job is successfully executed? Customers must keep an eye on the results or output during execution, especially to determine whether they have to make adjustments to get the task back on track in the event of a problem. For some jobs, customers must also monitor environmental factors to see whether and when adjustments are necessary. A network administrator, for example, monitors Web traffic to avoid system overload.

While some monitoring activities are passive (like the way a pacemaker monitors heartbeats), others can often be time-consuming and demanding for customers. When the costs of poor execution are significant, as when operating on a patient, solutions that call attention to problems or relevant changes in the environment are especially valuable. Solutions that link monitoring with improved job execution or that provide diagnostic feedback offer considerable value as well. Consider how Nike helps runners monitor their workouts using the Nike+iPod Sport Kit. A sensor placed in Nike shoes communicates with an iPod being worn by the runner, providing ongoing audio feedback about time, distance, pace, and calories burned. When the runner notices he is flagging, he can select his "power song" to reinvigorate himself. The kit also allows runners to track progress against predefined goals.

## 7: Modify

What might the customer need to alter for the job to be completed successfully? When there are changes in inputs or in the environment, or if the execution is problematic, the customer may need help with updates, adjustments, or maintenance. At this step, customers need help deciding what should be adjusted as well as determining when, how, and where to make changes. Like monitoring, searching for the right adjustment can be both time-consuming and costly. Companies can help by offering ways to get execution back on track when there are problems. They can also provide avenues for reducing the time needed make updates and the number of adjustments the customer has to make to achieve desired results. (In addition, solutions that target the location and preparation steps can be designed to eliminate modifications.) Many software programs perform well at supporting this step. Microsoft, for example, assists customers with the job of modifying their computer to protect against security threats. Automatic updates of its operating system remove the hassle of determining which updates are necessary, finding them, and ensuring that fixes are compatible with various elements of the operating system.

## 8: Conclude

What must the customer do to finish the job? With some simple jobs such as hand washing, the conclusion is self-evident. Complex jobs, on the other hand, may involve some concluding process steps. The office worker has to retrieve a document from the printer and possibly collate, bind, and store it. An anesthesiologist must document surgery details, as well as wake and oversee transfer of the patient to a postoperative recovery area.

Customers often think of concluding steps as burdensome because the core job has already been completed, so companies need to help them simplify the process. Also, the conclusion of one job cycle is often the start of another or may affect the next one's beginning. When a job is cyclical, companies can help customers make sure that concluding activities are closely connected to the starting point of a new job cycle.

One way to help customers finish the job is to design benefits sought at the conclusion into an earlier step in the process. 3M's Coban Self-Adherent Wrap, for example, offers a convenient way for medical personnel to secure wound dressings at the end of treatment, because it is made of a material that stretches and adheres only to itself. This self-adherence property makes the wrap easy to remove, because it doesn't stick to patient skin or the wound. 3M designed the product in such a way that putting on the wrap anticipates the act of taking it off.

## Ancillary Step: Troubleshooting

What problems must the customer troubleshoot and resolve in the course of performing the job? Even in the simplest jobs, things occasionally go wrong—orders are late, printers jam, surgical tools are misplaced, and software test cases fail. When that happens, the customer must disengage from the core job process and enter into a distinct ancillary job of troubleshooting and resolving the problem at hand. What customers want at that point is a speedy resolution— which is a function of how clearly the problem is understood. If the printer jams, for example, how should the office worker remove the damaged paper? If a nurse gets cut when a surgeon hands him a scalpel, what steps must the nurse take to avoid being infected with a blood-borne organism?

When a problem arises, customers need resources, tools, and diagnostics to help them determine a resolution quickly, protect themselves and resources that might be affected, and know when the problem is fixed. They also want solutions that prevent problems at each job step. Consider how MasterCard helps customers with the job of paying for products and services when problems occur. In addition to its zero-liability coverage policy, MasterCard provides downloadable contact numbers so that customers who lose a card while traveling know exactly how to contact the company to report the loss. Then MasterCard can send out emergency cash advances and a replacement card within 48 hours.

---

To identify opportunities for innovation, some companies focus on product leadership, some on operational excellence, and some on customer intimacy. Some offer services; others offer goods.

Regardless of which business model a company chooses, the fundamental basis for identifying opportunities for growth is the same. When companies understand that customers hire products, services, software, and ideas to get jobs done, they can dissect those jobs to discover the innovation opportunities that are the key to growth.

**Originally published in May 2008. Reprint R0805H**

# Is It Real? Can We Win? Is It Worth Doing?

Managing Risk and Reward in an Innovation Portfolio.
*by George S. Day*

MINOR INNOVATIONS MAKE up 85% to 90% of companies' development portfolios, on average, but they rarely generate the growth companies seek. At a time when companies should be taking bigger—but smart—innovation risks, their bias is in the other direction. From 1990 to 2004 the percentage of major innovations in development portfolios dropped from 20.4 to 11.5—even as the number of growth initiatives rose.[1] The result is internal traffic jams of safe, incremental innovations that delay all projects, stress organizations, and fail to achieve revenue goals.

These small projects, which I call "little i" innovations, are necessary for continuous improvement, but they don't give companies a competitive edge or contribute much to profitability. It's the risky "Big I" projects—new to the company or new to the world—that push the firm into adjacent markets or novel technologies and can generate the profits needed to close the gap between revenue forecasts and growth goals. (According to one study, only 14% of new-product launches were substantial innovations, but they accounted for 61% of all profit from innovations among the companies examined.)[2]

The aversion to Big I projects stems from a belief that they are too risky and their rewards (if any) will accrue too far in the future. Certainly the probability of failure rises sharply when a company ventures beyond incremental initiatives within familiar markets. But avoiding risky projects altogether can strangle growth. The solution is to pursue a disciplined, systematic process that will distribute your innovations more evenly across the spectrum of risk.

Two tools, used in tandem, can help companies do this. The first, the risk matrix, will graphically reveal risk exposure across an entire innovation portfolio. The second, the R-W-W ("real, win, worth it") screen, originated by Dominick ("Don") M. Schrello, of Long Beach, California, can be used to evaluate individual projects. Versions of the screen have been circulating since the 1980s, and since then a growing roster of companies, including General Electric, Honeywell, Novartis, Millipore, and 3M, have used them to assess business potential and risk exposure in their innovation portfolios; 3M has used R-W-W for more than 1,500 projects. I have expanded the screen and used it to evaluate dozens of projects at four global companies, and I have taught executives and Wharton students how to use it as well.

Although both tools, and the steps within them, are presented sequentially here, their actual use is not always linear. The information derived from each one can often be reapplied in later stages of development, and the two tools may inform each other. Usually, development teams quickly discover when and how to improvise on the tools' structured approach in order to maximize learning and value.

## The Risk Matrix

To balance its innovation portfolio, a company needs a clear picture of how its projects fall on the spectrum of risk. The risk matrix employs a unique scoring system and calibration of risk to help estimate the probability of success or failure for each project based on how big a stretch it is for the firm: The less familiar the intended market (x axis) and the product or technology (y axis), the higher the risk. (See the exhibit "Assessing risk across an innovation portfolio.")

# Idea in Brief

Incremental innovations (small, safe changes to your firm's offerings) make up 85%–90% of companies' development portfolios. But "little i" projects rarely produce competitive advantage. For that, you need "Big I" innovations—offerings new to your organization or the world. Yes, they're risky. But avoid them, and you may strangle your company's growth.

Day recommends a solution: Increase the proportion of major innovations in your portfolio while carefully managing their risks. Two tools can help:

- A **risk matrix** enables you to estimate each project's probability of success or failure based on how big a stretch it is for your firm. The less familiar the intended market and the product or technology, the higher the risk.

- The **R-W-W ("real," "win," "worth it") screen** helps you evaluate projects' feasibility. The first step in using this tool—asking "Is it real" questions—helps you determine whether customers want your innovation and, if so, whether you can build it.

A project's position on the matrix is determined by its score on a range of factors, such as how closely the behavior of targeted customers will match that of the company's current customers, how relevant the company's brand is to the intended market, and how applicable its technology capabilities are to the new product.

A portfolio review team—typically consisting of senior managers with strategic oversight and authority over development budgets and allocations—conducts the evaluation, with the support of each project's development team. Team members rate each project independently and then explain their rationale. They discuss reasons for any differences of opinion and seek consensus. The resulting scores serve as a project's coordinates on the risk matrix.

The determination of each score requires deep insights. When McDonald's attempted to offer pizza, for example, it assumed that the new offering was closely adjacent to its existing ones, and thus targeted its usual customers. Under that assumption, pizza would be a familiar product for the present market and would appear in the bottom left of the risk matrix. But the project failed, and a postmortem showed that the launch had been fraught with risk: Because

# Idea in Practice

## Using the Risk Matrix

Assemble a team to assess each innovation project's potential risk using these criteria:

- How closely target customers' behavior will match current customers'

- How relevant the company's brand is to the intended market

- How applicable your capabilities are to the new product

Neglect to assess risk, and you may make a major misstep.

*Example:* When McDonald's started offering pizza, it assumed the new product was closely adjacent to existing ones. So it targeted its usual customers. But employees couldn't make and serve a pizza within 30 seconds—which violated McDonald's service-delivery model. And the company's brand didn't give "permission" to offer pizza. The project failed.

## Using the R-W-W screen

Used throughout a product's development, the R-W-W screen exposes faulty assumptions, knowledge gaps, sources of risk, and problems suggesting termination. To employ this tool, repeatedly test each project's viability according to these criteria:

### Is it real?

| A **market** exists for the product if: | The **product** is real if: |
| --- | --- |
| • There's a need or desire for the product. | • It has precisely described characteristics. |
| • Customers can buy it (for example, they have the money). | • It can be produced with available technology and materials. |
| • There are enough potential buyers. | • It will satisfy the market in its final form. |
| • Consumers will buy (for instance, they're willing to switch to your offering). | |

### Can we win?

| The **product** will be competitive if: | Your **company** will be competitive if: |
|---|---|
| • It offers clear advantages over alternatives, such as greater safety or social acceptability (think hybrid cars).<br><br>• Those advantages can be sustained (for example, through patents).<br><br>• It can survive competitors' responses (such as a price war). | • It has superior resources (such as engineering or logistics).<br><br>• Managers have experience in the market and skills appropriate for the project's scale and complexity.<br><br>• Projects have champions who can energize development teams, sell the vision to senior management, and overcome adversity.<br><br>• It has mastery of market research tools and shares customers' insights with development-team members. |

### Is it worth doing?

| The product will be **profitable** at an acceptable risk if: | The product makes **strategic sense** if: |
|---|---|
| • Its forecasted returns are greater than costs—considering matters such as the timing and amount of capital outlays, marketing expenses, breakeven time, and the cost of product extensions needed to keep ahead of competitors. | • It fits with your company's growth strategy; for example, by enhancing customer relationships or creating opportunities for follow-on business. |

## Assessing risk across an innovation portfolio

### The risk matrix*

*This tool will reveal the distribution of risk across a company's innovation portfolio. Each innovation can be positioned on the matrix by determining its score on two dimensions—how familiar to the company the intended market is (x axis) and how familiar the product or technology is (y axis)—using the grid "Positioning projects on the matrix." Familiar products aimed at the company's current markets will fall in the bottom left of the matrix, indicating a low probability of failure. New products aimed at unfamiliar markets will fall in the upper right, revealing a high probability of failure.*

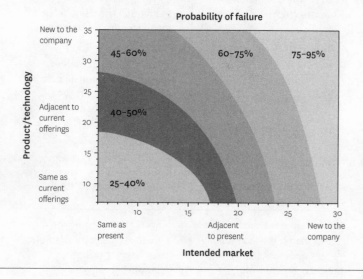

no one could figure out how to make and serve a pizza in 30 seconds or less, orders caused long backups, violating the McDonald's service-delivery model. The postmortem also revealed that the company's brand didn't give "permission" to offer pizza. Even though its core fast-food customers were demographically similar to pizza lovers, their expectations about the McDonald's experience didn't include pizza.

## Risk and revenue

*Each dot on this risk matrix stands for one innovation in an imaginary company's portfolio. The size of each dot is proportional to the project's estimated revenue. (Companies may choose to illustrate estimated development investment or some other financial measure instead.) This portfolio, dominated by relatively low-risk, low-reward projects, is typical in its distribution.*

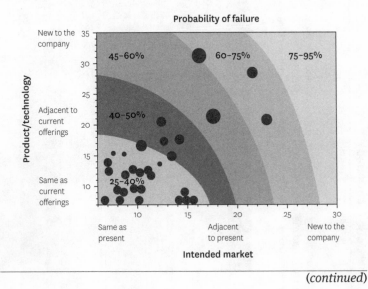

*(continued)*

Once the risk matrix has been completed, it typically reveals two things: that a company has more projects than it can manage well, and that the distribution of Big I and little i innovations is lopsided. Most companies will find that the majority of their projects cluster in the bottom left quadrant of the matrix, and a minority skew toward the upper right.

This imbalance is unhealthy if unsurprising. Discounted cash flow analysis and other financial yardsticks for evaluating development projects are usually biased against the delayed payoffs and uncertainty inherent in Big I innovations. What's more, little i projects tend to drain R&D budgets as companies struggle to keep up

# Assessing risk across an innovation portfolio (continued)

## Positioning projects on the matrix

*Position each innovation product or concept by completing each statement in the left-hand column with one of the options offered across the top to arrive at a score from 1 to 5. Add the six scores in the "Intended market" section to determine the project's x-axis coordinate. Add the seven scores in the "Product/technology" section to determine its y-axis coordinate.*

| | Intended market | | | | |
| --- | --- | --- | --- | --- | --- |
| | ...be the same as in our present market | | ...partially overlap with our present market | | ...be entirely different from our present market or are unknown |
| Customers' behavior and decision-making processes will... | 1 | 2 | 3 | 4 | 5 |
| Our distribution and sales activities will... | 1 | 2 | 3 | 4 | 5 |
| The competitive set (incumbents or potential entrants) will... | 1 | 2 | 3 | 4 | 5 |
| | ...highly relevant | | ...somewhat relevant | | ...not at all relevant |
| Our brand promise is... | 1 | 2 | 3 | 4 | 5 |
| Our current customer relationships are... | 1 | 2 | 3 | 4 | 5 |
| Our knowledge of competitors' behavior and intentions is... | 1 | 2 | 3 | 4 | 5 |
| | | | | | Total (x-axis coordinate) |

| Product/technology | | | | | |
|---|---|---|---|---|---|
| | ...is fully applicable | | ...will require significant adaptation | | ...is not applicable |
| Our current development capability... | 1 | 2 | 3 | 4 | 5 |
| Our technology competency... | 1 | 2 | 3 | 4 | 5 |
| Our intellectual property protection... | 1 | 2 | 3 | 4 | 5 |
| Our manufacturing and service delivery system... | 1 | 2 | 3 | 4 | 5 |
| | ...are identical to those of our current offerings | | ...overlap somewhat with those of our current offerings | | ...completely differ from those of our current offerings |
| The required knowledge and science bases... | 1 | 2 | 3 | 4 | 5 |
| The necessary product and service functions... | 1 | 2 | 3 | 4 | 5 |
| The expected quality standards... | 1 | 2 | 3 | 4 | 5 |
| | | | | | Total (y-axis coordinate) |

*This risk matrix was developed from many sources, including long-buried consulting reports by A.T. Kearney and other firms, the extensive literature on the economic performance of acquisitions and alliances, and numerous audits of product and service innovations. It broadly defines "failure" as significantly missing the objectives that were used to justify the investment in the growth initiative. Estimates of the probability of failure have been thoroughly validated in dozens of interviews with consultants and senior managers involved in innovation initiatives and are consistent with recent surveys that place the overall failure rate of new products close to 40%. The ranges in probabilities take into account some of the variability in organizations' definitions of failure and in what constitutes a new market or technology for a given company. The probabilities do not apply to fast-moving consumer goods (where incremental innovations have high long-run failure rates) or ethical pharmaceuticals, and don't distinguish whether "new to the company" is also "new to the world." (Although these are distinct categories, in my experience most major new-to-the-company innovations are also new to the world; for the purposes of this article, they're considered to be broadly overlapping.) "Market" refers to customers, not geographies.

with customers' and salespeople's demands for a continuous flow of incrementally improved products. The risk matrix creates a visual starting point for an ongoing dialogue about the company's mix of projects and their fit with strategy and risk tolerance. The next step is to look closely at each project's prospects in the marketplace.

## Screening with R-W-W

The R-W-W screen is a simple but powerful tool built on a series of questions about the innovation concept or product, its potential market, and the company's capabilities and competition (see the exhibit "Screening for success"). It is not an algorithm for making go/no-go decisions but, rather, a disciplined process that can be employed at multiple stages of product development to expose faulty assumptions, gaps in knowledge, and potential sources of risk, and to ensure that every avenue for improvement has been explored. The R-W-W screen can be used to identify and help fix problems that are miring a project, to contain risk, and to expose problems that can't be fixed and therefore should lead to termination.

Innovation is inherently messy, nonlinear, and iterative. For simplicity, this article focuses on using the R-W-W screen in the early stages to test the viability of product concepts. In reality, however, a given product would be screened repeatedly during development—at the concept stage, during prototyping, and early in the launch planning. Repeated assessment allows screeners to incorporate increasingly detailed product, market, and financial analyses into the evaluation, yielding ever more accurate answers to the screening questions.

R-W-W guides a development team to dig deeply for the answers to six fundamental questions: *Is the market real? Is the product real? Can the product be competitive? Can our company be competitive? Will the product be profitable at an acceptable risk? Does launching the product make strategic sense?*

The development team answers these queries by exploring an even deeper set of supporting questions. The team determines where the answer to each question falls on a continuum ranging from definitely yes to definitely no. A definite no to any of the first

## Screening for success

*Each product concept in your company's innovation portfolio should be assessed by its development team using the R-W-W screen below. A definite yes or no answer to the first-column questions Is it real?, Can we win?, and Is it worth doing? requires digging deeply for robust answers to the supporting questions in the second and third columns. Often a team will answer maybe; its goal should be to investigate all possible avenues to converting no or maybe into yes. A definite no to any second-column question typically leads to termination of the project, since failure is all but certain. A definite no to any third-column question argues strongly against proceeding with development. (The full set of questions in columns two and three of the screen come from evaluations of more than 50 product failures within two companies I worked with by teams of auditors who asked, "What questions, properly answered, might have prevented the failure?")*

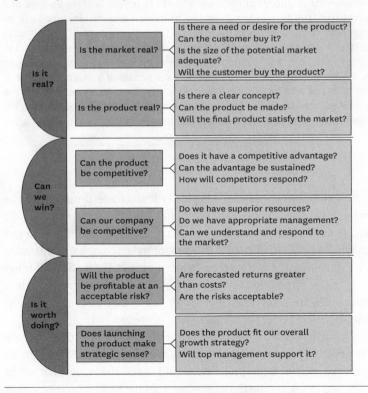

# The Screening Team

**PROJECT SCREENING TEAMS** vary by company, type of initiative, and stage of development. Over the course of R-W-W screening, teams typically involve members from across functions, including R&D, marketing, and manufacturing. They should also work with senior managers who are familiar with the screen and have the expertise and the instincts to push dispassionately for accurate answers, particularly at each decision point during development. At the same time, however, these managers should be sympathetic and willing to provide the team with the resources to fill information gaps.

A critical job in managing the R-W-W process is preventing teams from regarding the screen as an obstacle to be overcome or circumvented. It's also important that the team not regard the screen as simply a go/no-go tool imposed by management—a potential threat to a favorite project. Such a misperception will subvert proper use of the screen as a learning tool for revealing dubious assumptions and identifying problems and solutions.

Because the members of the development team are both evaluators and advocates, the screen is vulnerable to misuse and manipulation. Team members' convictions about the merits of the project may lead them to make cursory evaluations if they fear that a deep assessment, including a frank voicing of doubts, might imperil the project. One way to avoid this pitfall is to enlist a credible outside facilitator, perhaps someone from another part of the company who has a solid new-product track record and no stake in the outcome. This person's job should be to unearth all the key uncertainties, information gaps, and differences of opinion and help resolve them.

five fundamental questions typically leads to termination of the project, for obvious reasons. For example, if the consensus answer to *Can the product be competitive?* is a definite no, and the team can imagine no way to change it to a yes (or even a maybe), continuing with development is irrational. When a project has passed all other tests in the screen, however, and thus is a very good business bet, companies are sometimes more forgiving of a no to the sixth question, *Does launching the product make strategic sense?*

This article will delineate the screening process and demonstrate the depth of probing needed to arrive at valid answers. What follows is not, of course, a comprehensive guide to all the issues that might be raised by each question. Development teams can probe more or less deeply, as needed, at each decision point. (For more on team process, see the sidebar "The Screening Team.")

## Is It Real?

Figuring out whether a market exists and whether a product can be made to satisfy that market are the first steps in screening a product concept. Those steps will indicate the degree of opportunity for any firm considering the potential market, so the inquiring company can assess how competitive the environment might be right from the start.

One might think that asking if the envisioned product is even a possibility should come before investigating the potential market. But establishing that the market is real takes precedence for two reasons: First, the robustness of a market is almost always less certain than the technological ability to make something. This is one of the messages of the risk matrix, which shows that the probability of a product failure becomes greater when the *market* is unfamiliar to the company than when the *product or technology* is unfamiliar. A company's ability to crystallize the market concept—the target segment and how the product can do a better job of meeting its needs—is far more important than how well the company fields a fundamentally new product or technology. In fact, research by Procter & Gamble suggests that 70% of product failures across most categories occur because companies misconstrue the market. New Coke is a classic market-concept failure; Netflix got the market concept right. In each case the outcome was determined by the company's understanding of the market, not its facility with the enabling technologies.

Second, establishing the nature of the market can head off a costly "technology push." This syndrome often afflicts companies that emphasize how to solve a problem rather than what problem should be solved or what customer desires need to be satisfied. Segway, with its Personal Transporter, and Motorola, with its Iridium satellite phone, both succumbed to technology push. Segway's PT was an ingenious way to gyroscopically stabilize a two-wheeled platform, but it didn't solve the mobility problems of any target market. The reasons for Iridium's demise are much debated, but one possibility is that mobile satellite services proved less able than terrestrial wireless roaming services to cost-effectively meet the needs of most travelers.

Whether the market and the product are real should dominate the screening dialogue early in the development process, especially for Big I innovations. In the case of little i innovations, a close alternative will already be on the market, which has been proved to be real.

### Is the market real?

A market opportunity is real only when four conditions are satisfied: The proposed product will clearly meet a need or solve a problem better than available alternatives; customers are able to buy it; the potential market is big enough to be worth pursuing; and customers are willing to buy the product.

*Is there a need or desire for the product?* Unmet or poorly satisfied needs must be surfaced through market research using observational, ethnographic, and other tools to explore customers' behaviors, desires, motivations, and frustrations. Segway's poor showing is partly a market-research failure; the company didn't establish at the outset that consumers actually had a need for a self-balancing two-wheeled transporter.

Once a need has been identified, the next question is, *Can the customer buy it?* Even if the proposed product would satisfy a need and offer superior value, the market isn't real when there are objective barriers to purchasing it. Will budgetary constraints prevent customers from buying? (Teachers and school boards, for example, are always eager to invest in educational technologies but often can't find the funding.) Are there regulatory requirements that the new product may not meet? Are customers bound by contracts that would prevent them from switching to a new product? Could manufacturing or distribution problems prevent them from obtaining it?

The team next needs to ask, *Is the size of the potential market adequate?* It's dangerous to venture into a "trombone oil" market, where the product may provide distinctive value that satisfies a need, but the need is minuscule. A market opportunity isn't real unless there are enough potential buyers to warrant developing the product.

Finally, having established customers' need and ability to buy, the team must ask, *Will the customer buy the product?* Are there subjective barriers to purchasing it? If alternatives to the product exist, customers will evaluate them and consider, among other things, whether the new product delivers greater value in terms of features, capabilities, or cost. Improved value doesn't necessarily mean more capabilities, of course. Many Big I innovations, such as the Nintendo Wii, home defibrillators, and Salesforce.com's CRM software as a service, have prevailed by outperforming the incumbents on a few measures while being merely adequate on others. By the same token, some Big I innovations have stumbled because although they had novel capabilities, customers didn't find them superior to the incumbents.

Even when customers have a clear need or desire, old habits, the perception that a switch is too much trouble, or a belief that the purchase is risky can inhibit them. One company encountered just such a problem during the launch of a promising new epoxy for repairing machine parts during routine maintenance. Although the product could prevent costly shutdowns and thus offered unique value, the plant engineers and production managers at whom it was targeted vetoed its use. The engineers wanted more proof of the product's efficacy, while the production managers feared that it would damage equipment. Both groups were risk avoiders. A postmortem of the troubled launch revealed that maintenance people, unlike plant engineers and production managers, like to try new solutions. What's more, they could buy the product independently out of their own budgets, circumventing potential vetoes from higher up. The product was relaunched targeting maintenance and went on to become successful, but the delay was expensive and could have been avoided with better screening.

Customers may also be inhibited by a belief that the product will fail to deliver on its promise or that a better alternative might soon become available. Addressing this reluctance requires foresight into the possibilities of improvement among competitors. The prospects of third-generation (3G) mobile phones were dampened by enhancements in 2.5G phones, such as high-sensitivity antennae that made the incumbent technology perform much better.

### Is the product real?

Once a company has established the reality of the market, it should look closely at the product concept and expand its examination of the intended market.

*Is there a clear concept?* Before development begins, the technology and performance requirements of the concept are usually poorly defined, and team members often have diverging ideas about the product's precise characteristics. This is the time to expose those ideas and identify exactly what is to be developed. As the project progresses and the team becomes immersed in market realities, the requirements should be clarified. This entails not only nailing down technical specifications but also evaluating the concept's legal, social, and environmental acceptability.

*Can the product be made?* If the concept is solid, the team must next explore whether a viable product is feasible. Could it be created with available technology and materials, or would it require a breakthrough of some sort? If the product can be made, can it be produced and delivered cost-effectively, or would it be so expensive that potential customers would shun it? Feasibility also requires either that a value chain for the proposed product exists or that it can be easily and affordably developed, and that de facto technology standards (such as those ensuring compatibility among products) can be met.

Some years ago the R-W-W screen was used to evaluate a radical proposal to build nuclear power–generating stations on enormous floating platforms moored offshore. Power companies were drawn to the idea, because it solved both cooling and not-in-my-backyard problems. But the team addressing the *Is the product real?* stage of the process found that the inevitable flexing of the giant platforms would lead to metal fatigue and joint wear in pumps and turbines. Since this problem was deemed insurmountable, the team concluded that absent some technological breakthrough, the no answer to the feasibility question could never become even a maybe, and development was halted.

*Will the final product satisfy the market?* During development, trade-offs are made in performance attributes; unforeseen technical, manufacturing, or systems problems arise; and features are modified. At each such turn in the road, a product designed to meet customer expectations may lose some of its potential appeal. Failure to monitor these shifts can result in the launch of an offering that looked great on the drawing board but falls flat in the marketplace.

Consider the ongoing disappointment of e-books. Even though the newest entrant, the Sony Reader, boasts a huge memory and breakthrough display technology, using it doesn't begin to compare with the experience of reading conventional books. The promised black-on-white effect is closer to dark gray on light gray. Meanwhile, the Reader's unique features, such as the ability to store many volumes and to search text, are for many consumers insufficiently attractive to offset the near $300 price tag. Perhaps most important, consumers are well satisfied with ordinary books. By July of 2007 the entire e-book category had reached only $30 million in sales for the year.

## Can We Win?

After determining that the market and the product are both real, the project team must assess the company's ability to gain and hold an adequate share of the market. Simply finding a real opportunity doesn't guarantee success: The more real the opportunity, the more likely it is that hungry competitors are eyeing it. And if the market is already established, incumbents will defend their positions by copying or leapfrogging any innovations.

Two of the top three reasons for new-product failures, as revealed by audits, would have been exposed by the *Can we win?* analysis: Either the new product didn't achieve its market-share goals, or prices dropped much faster than expected. (The third reason is that the market was smaller, or grew more slowly, than expected.)

The questions at this stage of the R-W-W screening carefully distinguish between the offering's ability to succeed in the marketplace and the company's capacity—through resources and management talent—to help it do so.

## Can the product be competitive?

Customers will choose one product over alternatives if it's perceived as delivering superior value with some combination of benefits such as better features, lower life-cycle cost, and reduced risk. The team must assess all sources of perceived value for a given product and consider the question *Does it have a competitive advantage?* (Here the customer research that informed the team's evaluation of whether the market and the product were real should be drawn on and extended as needed.) Can someone else's offering provide customers with the same results or benefits? One company's promising laminate technology, for instance, had intrigued technical experts, but the launch failed because the customers' manufacturing people had found other, cheaper ways to achieve the same improvement. The team should also consider whether the product offers additional tangible advantages—such as lifetime cost savings, greater safety, higher quality, and lower maintenance or support needs—or intangible benefits, such as greater social acceptability (think of hybrid cars and synthetic-fur coats) and the promise of reduced risk that is implicit in a trusted brand name.

*Can the advantage be sustained?* Competitive advantage is only as good as the company's ability to keep imitators at bay. The first line of defense is patents. The project team should evaluate the relevance of its existing patents to the product in development and decide what additional patents may be needed to protect related intellectual property. It should ask whether a competitor could reverse engineer the product or otherwise circumvent patents that are essential to the product's success. If maintaining advantage lies in tacit organizational knowledge, can that knowledge be protected? For example, how can the company ensure that the people who have it will stay? What other barriers to imitation are possible? Can the company lock up scarce resources or enter into exclusive supply contracts?

Consider the case of 3M's computer privacy screen. Although the company's microlouver technology promised unique privacy benefits, its high price threatened to limit sales to a small market niche, making the project's status uncertain. An R-W-W screening, however, revealed that the technology was aggressively patented, so no competitor could imitate its performance. It also clarified an opportunity in adjacent markets for antiglare filters for computers. Armed with these insights, 3M used the technology to launch a full line of privacy and antiglare screens while leveraging its brand equity and sales presence in the office-products market. Five years later the product line formed the basis of one of 3M's fastest-growing businesses.

*How will competitors respond?* Assuming that patent protection is (or will be) in place, the project team needs to investigate competitive threats that patents can't deflect. A good place to start is a "red team" exercise: If we were going to attack our own product, what vulnerabilities would we find? How can we reduce them? A common error companies make is to assume that competitors will stand still while the new entrant fine-tunes its product prior to launch. Thus the team must consider what competing products will look like when the offering is introduced, how competitors may react after the launch, and how the company could respond. Finally, the team should examine the possible effects of this competitive interplay on prices. Would the product survive a sustained price war?

### Can our company be competitive?

After establishing that the offering can win, the team must determine whether or not the company's resources, management, and market insight are better than those of the competition. If not, it may be impossible to sustain advantage, no matter how good the product.

*Do we have superior resources?* The odds of success increase markedly when a company has or can get resources that both enhance customers' perception of the new product's value and surpass those of competitors. Superior engineering, service delivery, logistics, or brand equity can give a new product an edge by better meeting customers' expectations. The European no-frills airline easyJet, for example, has successfully expanded into cruises and car rentals by leveraging its ability to blend convenience, low cost, and market-appropriate branding to appeal to small-business people and other price-sensitive travelers.

If the company doesn't have superior resources, addressing the deficiency is often straightforward. When the U.S. market leader for high-efficiency lighting products wanted to expand into the local-government market, for example, it recognized two barriers: The company was unknown to the buyers, and it had no experience with the competitive bidding process they used. It overcame these problems by hiring people who were skilled at analyzing competitors, anticipating their likely bids, and writing proposals. Some of these people came from the competition, which put the company's rivals at a disadvantage.

Sometimes, though, deficiencies are more difficult to overcome, as is the case with brand equity. As part of its inquiry into resources, the project team must ask whether the company's brand provides— or denies—permission to enter the market. The 3M name gave a big boost to the privacy screen because it is strongly associated with high-quality, innovative office supplies—whereas the McDonald's name couldn't stretch to include pizza. Had the company's management asked whether its brand equity was both relevant and superior to that of the competition—such as Papa Gino's—the answer would have been equivocal at best.

*Do we have appropriate management?* Here the team must examine whether the organization has direct or related experience with the market, whether its development-process skills are appropriate for the scale and complexity of the project, and whether the project both fits company culture and has a suitable champion. Success requires a passionate cheerleader who will energize the team, sell the vision to senior management, and overcome skepticism or adversity along the way. But because enthusiasm can blind champions to potentially crippling faults and lead to a biased search for evidence that confirms a project's viability, their advocacy must be constructively challenged throughout the screening process.

*Can we understand and respond to the market?* Successful product development requires a mastery of market-research tools, an openness to customer insights, and the ability to share them with development-team members. Repeatedly seeking the feedback of potential customers to refine concepts, prototypes, and pricing ensures that products won't have to be recycled through the development process to fix deficiencies.

Most companies wait until after development to figure out how to price the new product—and then sometimes discover that customers won't pay. Procter & Gamble avoids this problem by including pricing research early in the development process. It also asks customers to actually buy products in development. Their answers to *whether* they would buy are not always reliable predictors of future purchasing behavior.

## Is It Worth Doing?

Just because a project can pass the tests up to this point doesn't mean it is worth pursuing. The final stage of the screening provides a more rigorous analysis of financial and strategic value.

### Will the product be profitable at an acceptable risk?

Few products launch unless top management is persuaded that the answer to *Are forecasted returns greater than costs?* is definitely yes. This requires projecting the timing and amount of capital outlays, marketing expenses, costs, and margins; applying time to breakeven, cash flow, net present value, and other standard financial-performance measures; and estimating the profitability and cash flow from both aggressive and cautious launch plans. Financial projections should also include the cost of product extensions and enhancements needed to keep ahead of the competition.

Forecasts of financial returns from new products are notoriously unreliable. Project managers know they are competing with other worthy projects for scarce resources and don't want theirs to be at a disadvantage. So it is not surprising that project teams' financial reports usually meet upper management's financial-performance requirements. Given the susceptibility of financial forecasts to manipulation, overconfidence, and bias, executives should depend on rigorous answers to the prior questions in the screen for their conclusions about profitability.

*Are the risks acceptable?* A forecast's riskiness can be initially assessed with a standard sensitivity test: How will small changes in price, market share, and launch timing affect cash flows and breakeven points? A big change in financial results stemming from a small one in input assumptions indicates a high degree of risk. The financial analysis should consider opportunity costs: Committing resources to one project may hamper the development of others.

To understand risk at a deeper level, consider all the potential causes of product failure that have been unearthed by the R-W-W screen and devise ways to mitigate them—such as partnering with a company that has market or technology expertise your firm lacks.

### Does launching the product make strategic sense?

Even when a market and a concept are real, the product and the company could win, and the project would be profitable, it may not make strategic sense to launch. To evaluate the strategic rationale for development, the project team should ask two more questions.

*Does the product fit our overall growth strategy?* In other words, will it enhance the company's capabilities by, for example, driving the expansion of manufacturing, logistics, or other functions? Will it have a positive or a negative impact on brand equity? Will it cannibalize or improve sales of the company's existing products? (If the former, is it better to cannibalize one's own products than to lose sales to competitors?) Will it enhance or harm relationships with stakeholders—dealers, distributors, regulators, and so forth? Does the project create opportunities for follow-on business or new markets that would not be possible otherwise? (Such an opportunity helped 3M decide to launch its privacy screen: The product had only a modest market on its own, but the launch opened up a much bigger market for antiglare filters.) These questions can serve as a starting point for what must be a thorough evaluation of the product's strategic fit. A discouraging answer to just one of them shouldn't kill a project outright, but if the overall results suggest that a project makes little strategic sense, the launch is probably ill-advised.

*Will top management support it?* It's certainly encouraging for a development team when management commits to the initial concept. But the ultimate success of a project is better assured if management signs on because the project's assumptions can withstand the rigorous challenges of the R-W-W screen.

**Notes**

1. Robert G. Cooper, "Your NPD Portfolio May Be Harmful to Your Business Health," *PDMA Visions,* April 2005.

2. W. Chan Kim and Renée Mauborgne, "Strategy, Value Innovation, and the Knowledge Economy," *Sloan Management Review,* Spring 1999.

**Originally published in December 2007. Reprint R0712S**

# Six Myths of Product Development

The Fallacies That Cause Delays,
Undermine Quality, and Raise Costs.
*by Stefan Thomke and*
*Donald Reinertsen*

**MOST PRODUCT-DEVELOPMENT MANAGERS** are always struggling to bring in projects on time and on budget. They never have enough resources to get the job done, and their bosses demand predictable schedules and deliverables. So the managers push their teams to be more parsimonious, to write more-detailed plans, and to minimize schedule variations and waste. But that approach, which may work well in turning around underperforming factories, can actually hurt product-development efforts.

Although many companies treat product development as if it were similar to manufacturing, the two are profoundly different. In the world of manufacturing physical objects, tasks are repetitive, activities are reasonably predictable, and the items being created can be in only one place at a time. In product development many tasks are unique, project requirements constantly change, and the output—thanks, in part, to the widespread use of advanced computer-aided design and simulation and the incorporation of software in physical products—is information, which can reside in multiple places at the same time.

The failure to appreciate those critical differences has given rise to several fallacies that undermine the planning, execution, and evaluation of product-development projects. Together, we have spent more than 50 years studying and advising companies on product-development efforts, and we have encountered these misconceptions—as well as others that arise for different reasons—in a wide range of industries, including semiconductors, autos, consumer electronics, medical devices, software, and financial services. In this article we'll expose them and offer ways to overcome the problems they create.

## Fallacy 1: High Utilization of Resources Will Improve Performance

In both our research and our consulting work, we've seen that the vast majority of companies strive to fully employ their product-development resources. (One of us, Donald, through surveys conducted in executive courses at the California Institute of Technology, has found that the average product-development manager keeps capacity utilization above 98%.) The logic seems obvious: Projects take longer when people are not working 100% of the time—and therefore, a busy development organization will be faster and more efficient than one that is not as good at utilizing its people.

But in practice that logic doesn't hold up. We have seen that projects' speed, efficiency, and output quality inevitably decrease when managers completely fill the plates of their product-development employees—no matter how skilled those managers may be. High utilization has serious negative side effects, which managers underestimate for three reasons.

### They don't take into full account the intrinsic variability of development work
Many aspects of product development are unpredictable: when projects will arrive, what individual tasks they'll require, and how long it will take workers who've never tackled such tasks before to do them. Companies, however, are most familiar with repetitive

# Idea in Brief

Many companies approach product development as if it were manufacturing, trying to control costs and improve quality by applying zero-defect, efficiency-focused techniques. While this tactic can boost the performance of factories, it generally backfires with product development. The process of designing products is profoundly different from the process of making them, and the failure of executives to appreciate the differences leads to several fallacies that actually hurt product-development efforts.

In this article, the authors, an HBS professor and a consultant, expose these misperceptions and others. They look at six dangerous myths:

1. High utilization of resources will make the department more efficient.

2. Processing work in large batches will be more economical.

3. Teams need to faithfully follow their development plan, minimizing any deviations from it.

4. The sooner a project is started, the sooner it will be finished.

5. The more features a product has, the better customers will like it.

6. Projects will be more successful if teams "get them right the first time."

The authors explain the negative effects these "principles" have when applied to product development, offer practical guidelines on overcoming them, and walk readers through a visual tool that will help them keep projects on track.

processes like manufacturing and transaction processing, where the work doesn't change much and surprises are few and far between. Such processes behave in an orderly manner as the utilization of resources increases. Add 5% more work, and it will take 5% more time to complete.

Processes with high variability behave very differently. As utilization increases, delays lengthen dramatically. (See the exhibit "High utilization leads to delays.") Add 5% more work, and completing it may take 100% longer. But few people understand this effect. In our experience with hundreds of product-development teams, we have found that most were significantly overcommitted. To complete all projects on time and on budget, some organizations we worked with would have needed at least 50% more resources than they had.

## High utilization leads to delays

*The curve below is calculated using Queuing Theory, the mathematical study of waiting lines. It shows that with variable processes, the amount of time projects spend on hold, waiting to be worked on, rises steeply as utilization of resources increases. Though the curve changes slightly depending on the project work, it always turns sharply upward as utilization nears 100%.*

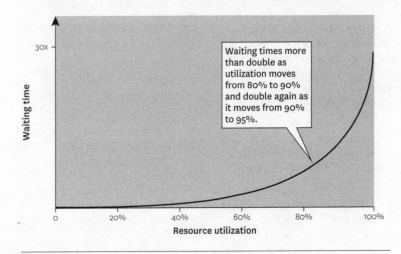

It is true that some variability is the result of a lack of discipline, and that some product-development tasks (like designing components for an airplane prototype or performing clinical trials) include more-repetitive work. But even if some of the work is predictable, when it's combined with other unpredictable work, you will see queuing problems.

### They don't understand how queues affect economic performance

High utilization of resources inevitably creates queues of projects. When partially completed work sits idle, waiting for capacity to become available, the duration of the overall project will grow. Queues also delay feedback, causing developers to follow unproductive paths longer. They make it hard for companies to adjust to evolving market needs and to detect weaknesses in their product before it's too late. Ironically, these problems are precisely the ones that managers think high utilization will allow their teams to avoid.

Even when managers know that they're creating queues, they rarely realize the economic cost. Although that cost can be quantified, we've found that the vast majority of companies don't calculate it. Managers need to weigh queue costs against the costs of underutilized capacity in order to strike the right balance.

### In product development, work-in-process inventory is predominantly invisible

Manufacturing queues consist of physical things, and when inventory in a factory doubles, it's obvious. That's not the case in product development, where inventory largely consists of information, such as design documentation, test procedures and results, and instructions for building prototypes. When inventory doubles in an engineering process, there are no physical signs. Moreover, because accounting standards require most R&D inventory to be carried at zero value, financial statements give no indication of serious inventory excesses in product development.

It is very difficult to fight a problem that you can't see or measure. Consider the situation at a major pharmaceutical firm. Several years ago its newly appointed head of drug discovery faced a managerial dilemma. Like other senior executives who run large R&D organizations, he was trying to find ways to make his scientists more innovative. He wanted them to experiment more with new chemical compounds that could generate promising new drugs and, at the same time, to eliminate unpromising candidates as early as possible. Experiments with living organisms, however, were the responsibility of animal testing, a department that was not under his control and was run as a cost center. It was evaluated by how efficiently it used testing resources, which naturally led to high utilization. Consequently, the scientists in drug discovery had to wait three to four months for the results of tests that took a little more than a week to perform. The "well-managed" testing organization impeded the discovery unit's progress.

The obvious solution to such problems is to provide a capacity buffer in processes that are highly variable. Some companies have long understood this. For decades, 3M has scheduled product developers at 85% of their capacity. And Google is famous for its "20% time" (allowing engineers to work one day a week on anything they want—a practice that means extra capacity is available if a project falls behind schedule). However, in our experience this kind of solution is quite hard to implement. As we will discuss, few organizations can resist the temptation to use every last bit of available capacity. Managers reflexively start more work whenever they see idle time.

But there are other viable solutions:

**Change the management-control systems.** For the pharmaceutical company, this might involve taking steps to align the objectives of the animal-testing unit with those of the discovery unit. The company could, for example, reward animal testing for prompt responses (measuring time from request to completion of test) rather than resource utilization.

**Selectively increase capacity.** Adding extra resources to the areas where the utilization rates are 70% or higher can significantly reduce waiting time. If the pharmaceutical company did this in animal testing, it would obtain feedback on new chemical compounds far faster. In settings where testing is conducted with computer modeling and simulation, increasing capacity is often relatively inexpensive, since it just involves buying additional computer equipment and software licenses.

**Limit the number of active projects.** If the pharmaceutical firm couldn't increase animal testing's capacity, it could still lower the utilization rate by reducing the number of active projects exploring new chemical compounds. The discipline of putting a hard limit on what goes into a product-development pipeline often results in sharper focus and clearer priorities.

**Make the work-in-process inventory easier to see.** One method is to use visual control boards. These can take a number of forms, but the key is to have some sort of physical token, such as a Post-it note, represent the development work (see the exhibit "Typical work-in-process control board"). A control board should display all active work and show what state each part of the project is in. It should be at the center of the team's management process. Teams can hold 15-minute daily stand-up meetings around such boards to coordinate efforts and keep work moving.

## Fallacy 2: Processing Work in Large Batches Improves the Economics of the Development Process

A second cause of queues in product development is batch size. Let's say a new product is composed of 200 components. You could choose to design and build all 200 parts before you test any of them. If you instead designed and built only 20 components before you began testing, the batch size would be 90% smaller. That would have a profound effect on queue time, because the average queue in a process is directly proportional to batch size.

The reduction of batch sizes is a critical principle of lean manufacturing. Small batches allow manufacturers to slash work in process and accelerate feedback, which, in turn, improves cycle times, quality, and efficiency. Small batches have even greater utility in product development, but few developers realize the power of this method.

One reason is the nature of their work flow. Again, because the information they're producing is mostly invisible to them, the batch sizes are too. Second, developers seem to have an inherent bias to use large batches—possibly because they incorrectly believe that large batches produce economies of scale.

In a well-managed process, the batch size will balance transaction and holding costs (see the exhibit "How to determine optimal batch size"). It's similar to buying eggs at the grocery store. If you buy a 12-month supply on a single trip, your transaction cost is low, but most of the eggs will spoil, increasing your holding cost. If you buy a one-day supply at a time, your spoilage will be low, but your transaction costs will be high. Intuitively, you try to strike a balance between the two.

## How to determine optimal batch size

*Changes in batch size affect two primary costs: the transaction cost and the holding cost. As batch sizes become larger, average inventory levels rise, which raises holding costs. But at the same time, transaction costs decrease, because it takes fewer transactions to service demand.*

*The optimal batch size is the point where the total cost (combined holding and transaction cost) is lowest. When a company operates near this point, small deviations have little impact. For example, if a company operates at less than 20% above or below the optimal batch size, total costs increase less than 3%. So even rough estimates permit a company to capture large economic benefits.*

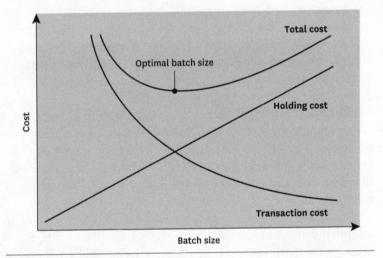

The companies that understand how this works have exploited IT advances to reduce batch sizes, often with astonishing results. Some software companies that used to test large batches of code every 90 days are now testing much smaller batches several times a day. A manufacturer of computer peripherals that used a similar approach with its software group reduced cycle time in software testing by 95% (from 48 months to 2.5 months), improved efficiency by 220%, and decreased defects by 33%. The cost savings were twice as high as the company had expected. Although those results were exceptional, we have found that reducing batch size improves most development projects significantly. Similarly, computerized modeling and simulation tools have dramatically lowered the optimal batch size of experimentation and testing in companies that develop physical products.

## Fallacy 3: Our Development Plan Is Great; We Just Need to Stick to It

In all our consulting work and research, we've never come across a single product-development project whose requirements remained stable throughout the design process. Yet many organizations place inordinate faith in their plans. They attribute any deviations to poor management and execution and, to minimize them, carefully track every step against intermediate targets and milestones. Such thinking is fine for highly repetitive activities in established manufacturing processes. But it can lead to poor results in product innovation, where new insights are generated daily and conditions are constantly changing.

A classic study of technical problem solving done by Thomas Allen of MIT highlights the fluid nature of development work. He found that engineers who were developing an aerospace subsystem conceived of and evaluated a number of design alternatives before selecting one that they judged to be the best. Along the way their preferences changed frequently, as they tested and refined competing technical solutions. This is typical in innovation projects: Testing and experimentation reveal what does and doesn't work, and initial assumptions about costs and value may be disproved.

Defining customers' needs can also be hard to do at the outset of a product-development project. When you think about it, that's not surprising: It isn't easy for customers to accurately specify their needs for solutions that don't yet exist. In fact, familiarity with existing product attributes can interfere with an individual's ability to express his or her need for a novel product. Customers' preferences can also shift abruptly during the course of a development project, as competitors introduce new offerings and new trends emerge.

For all those reasons, sticking to the original plan—no matter how excellent its conception and how skillful its execution—can be a recipe for disaster. This is not to suggest that we don't believe in planning. Product development is a set of complex activities that require careful coordination and attention to the smallest detail. However, the plan should be treated as an initial hypothesis that is constantly revised as the evidence unfolds, economic assumptions change, and the opportunity is reassessed. (See "The Value Captor's Process," by Rita Gunther McGrath and Thomas Keil, HBR May 2007.)

## Fallacy 4: The Sooner the Project Is Started, the Sooner It Will Be Finished

As we discussed earlier, idle time is anathema to managers. They tend to exploit any downtime by starting a new project. Even if the task cannot be completed because people have to return to another project, managers reason that anything accomplished on the new project is work that won't have to be done later. Such thinking leads companies to start more projects than they can vigorously pursue, diluting resources.

This dilution is dangerous. If a company embarks on a project before it has the resources to move ahead, it will stumble slowly through the development process. That's problematic because product-development work is highly perishable: Assumptions about technologies and the market can quickly become obsolete. The slower a project progresses, the greater the likelihood it will have to be redirected. Indeed, one branch of the military discovered that its cost and schedule overruns were exponentially proportional (to the fourth power) to a project's duration. In other words, when the original schedule of a project doubled, the cost and schedule overruns increased by a factor of 16.

The importance of reducing the amount of work in process is evident when we look at one of the classic formulas of queuing theory: Little's Law. It simply states that, on average, cycle time is proportional to the size of the queue divided by the processing rate. Thus,

## Typical work-in-process control board

*Control boards make invisible work visible by showing the precise stage that each work item is in. In designing the boards, most teams limit the number of tasks at each stage to prevent delays. This simple board contains features that might be found on a software project that involves a team composed of six to 10 people.*

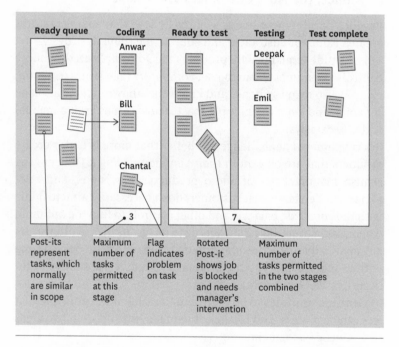

| Ready queue | Coding | Ready to test | Testing | Test complete |
| --- | --- | --- | --- | --- |
| | Anwar | | Deepak | |
| | Bill | | Emil | |
| | Chantal | | | |
| | 3 | 7 | | |

| Post-its represent tasks, which normally are similar in scope | Maximum number of tasks permitted at this stage | Flag indicates problem on task | Rotated Post-it shows job is blocked and needs manager's intervention | Maximum number of tasks permitted in the two stages combined |

if 20 people are ahead of you in line at Starbucks and the barista is serving five people a minute, you will be served in four minutes. You can shorten the cycle time by raising the processing rate or by reducing the number of jobs under way. In most settings the latter is the only practical choice.

For some product developers the solution has been to rigorously control the rate at which they start work. They match it to the rate at which work is actually completed; carefully manage the number of projects in process; make sure that once a project is launched, it is adequately staffed until it is completed; and resist the temptation to steal resources from an ongoing project to squeeze in new ones.

## Fallacy 5: The More Features We Put into a Product, the More Customers Will Like It

Product-development teams seem to believe that adding features creates value for customers and subtracting them destroys value. This attitude explains why products are so complicated: Remote controls seem impossible to use, computers take hours to set up, cars have so many switches and knobs that they resemble airplane cockpits, and even the humble toaster now comes with a manual and LCD displays.

Companies that challenge the belief that more is better create products that are elegant in their simplicity. Bang & Olufsen, the Danish manufacturer of audio products, televisions, and telephones, understands that customers don't necessarily want to fiddle with the equalizer, balance, and other controls to find the optimum combination of settings for listening to music. Its high-end speakers automatically make the adjustments needed to reproduce a song with as much fidelity to the original as possible. All that's left for users to select is the volume.

Getting companies to buy into and implement the principle that less can be more is hard because it requires extra effort in two areas of product development.

### Defining the problem

Articulating the problem that developers will try to solve is the most underrated part of the innovation process. Too many companies devote far too little time to it. But this phase is important because it's where teams develop a clear understanding of what their goals are and generate hypotheses that can be tested and refined through experiments. The quality of a problem statement makes all the difference in a team's ability to focus on the few features that really matter.

When Walt Disney was planning Disneyland, he didn't rush to add more features (rides, kinds of food, amount of parking) than other amusement parks had. Rather, he began by asking a much larger question: How could Disneyland provide visitors with a magical customer experience? Surely, the answer didn't come overnight; it required painstakingly detailed research, constant experimentation, and deep insights into what "magical" meant to Disney and its customers. IDEO and other companies have dedicated phases in which they completely immerse themselves in the context in which the envisioned product or service will be used. Their developers read everything of interest about the markets, observe and interview future users, research offerings that will compete with the new product, and synthesize everything that they have learned into pictures, models, and diagrams. The result is deep insights into customers that are tested, improved, or abandoned throughout the iterative development process.

### Determining what to hide or omit

Teams are often tempted to show off by producing brilliant technical solutions that amaze their peers and management. But often customers would prefer a product that just works effortlessly. From a customer's point of view, the best solutions solve a problem in the simplest way and hide the work that developers are so proud of.

One company that has understood this is Apple. It is known for many things—innovative products, stylish designs, and savvy marketing—but perhaps its greatest strength is its ability to get to the heart of a problem. (See "The Real Leadership Lessons of Steve Jobs," by Walter Isaacson, in our April issue.) As the late Steve Jobs once explained, "When you start looking at a problem and it seems really simple, you don't really understand the complexity of the problem. And your solutions are way too oversimplified. Then you get into the problem, and you see it's really complicated. And you come up with all these convoluted solutions. . . . That's where most people stop." Not Apple. It keeps on plugging away. "The really great person will keep on going," said Jobs, "and find . . . the key underlying principle of the problem and come up with a beautiful, elegant solution that works."

Determining which features to omit is just as important as—and perhaps more important than—figuring out which ones to include. Unfortunately, many companies, in an effort to be innovative, throw in every possible bell and whistle without fully considering important factors such as the value to customers and ease of use. When such companies do omit some planned functionality, it's typically because they need to cut costs or have fallen behind schedule or because the team has failed in some other way.

Instead, managers should focus on figuring out whether the deletion of any proposed feature might improve a particular product and allow the team to concentrate on things that truly heighten the overall customer experience. This can be determined by treating each alleged requirement as a hypothesis and testing it in small, quick experiments with prospective customers.

Development teams often assume that their products are done when no more features can be added. Perhaps their logic should be the reverse: Products get closer to perfection when no more features can be eliminated. As Leonardo da Vinci once said, "Simplicity is the ultimate sophistication."

## Fallacy 6: We Will Be More Successful If We Get It Right the First Time

Many product-development projects fail to meet their objectives for budgets, schedules, and technical performance. Undoubtedly, poor planning, rigid processes, and weak leadership all play a role. But another cause that's often overlooked is managers' demand that their teams "get it right the first time." Requiring success on the first pass biases teams toward the least-risky solutions, even if customers don't consider them much of an improvement over what's already available. Worse yet, teams have little incentive to pursue innovative solutions to customers' problems.

To avoid making mistakes, teams follow a linear process in which each stage (specify, design, build, test, scale, launch) is carefully monitored at review "gates." Work on the next stage cannot

## Practical guidelines for overcoming common fallacies

*A checklist for today's product-development managers*

1. Make queues and information flows visible.

2. Quantify the cost of delays and factor it into your decisions.

3. Introduce resource slack where utilization is highest.

4. Shift the focus of control systems from efficiency to response time.

5. Reduce transaction costs to enable smaller batch sizes and faster feedback.

6. Experiment with smaller batches; you can easily revert to large batches if this doesn't work.

7. Treat the development plan as a hypothesis that will evolve as new information becomes available.

8. Start projects only when you are ready to make a full commitment.

9. Aim for simplicity: Ask what features can be deleted, not just what can be added.

10. Experiment early, rapidly, and frequently, with computer models and physical prototypes, in controlled and real-life customer environments.

11. Emphasize overlapping and iterative—not linear—process designs.

12. Focus on quick feedback instead of first-pass success.

begin until the project passes through the gate. As the project moves down the line, significant commitments are made and the cost of responding to new insights increases by orders of magnitude. Successful tests in late stages are celebrated, and surprises, no matter how valuable they are, are considered setbacks. Unfortunately, such a linear process flow can cause project overruns because test feedback is delayed, teams cling to bad ideas longer than they should, and problems aren't unearthed until it's expensive to solve them.

A tolerance for "getting it wrong the first time" can be the better strategy as long as people iterate rapidly and frequently and learn quickly from their failures. Advances in simulation and rapid-prototyping technologies have made operating in this fashion vastly easier and less expensive.

Consider what we found in a study of 391 teams that designed custom integrated circuits. Teams that followed an iterative approach and conducted early and frequent tests made more errors along the way. But because they used low-cost prototyping technologies, they outperformed (in terms of the time and effort required) teams that tried to get their design right the first time. The teams that faced high prototyping costs invested more effort on specification, development, and verification. And because they did their iterations later in the process—and did far fewer of them—they delayed the discovery of critical problems.

Experimenting with many diverse ideas is crucial to innovation projects. When people experiment rapidly and frequently, many novel concepts will fail, of course. But such early failures can be desirable because they allow teams to eliminate poor options quickly and focus on more-promising alternatives. A crash test that shows that a car design is unsafe, a drug candidate that proves to be toxic, or a software user interface that confuses customers can all be desirable outcomes—provided that they occur early in a process, when few resources have been committed, designs are still very flexible, and other solutions can be tried.

A classic example of the advantages of the "fail early, fail often" approach is Team New Zealand's surprising victory in the 1995 America's Cup. To test ideas for improving the keel design, the team used two nearly identical boats: one boat that was modified during the course of the project and a "control" boat that was not. On a daily basis, the team simulated hypotheses on a local graphics workstation, applied those that looked promising to the one boat, raced it against the control, and analyzed the results. In contrast, its competitor, Team Dennis Conner, which had access to more-powerful computers (supercomputers at Boeing), ran large batches of simulations every few weeks and then tested possible solutions on one boat. The result: Team New Zealand completed many more learning cycles, eliminated unpromising ideas more rapidly, and ended up beating Team Dennis Conner's boat *Young America.*

What we hope is becoming clear by now is that experiments resulting in failures are not necessarily failed experiments. They generate new information that an innovator was unable to foresee. The faster the experimentation cycle, the more feedback can be gathered and incorporated into new rounds of experiments with novel and potentially risky ideas. In such an environment employees tend to persevere when times get tough, engage in more-challenging work, and outperform their risk-averse peers.

But creating this kind of environment isn't easy—a topic that Amy C. Edmondson of Harvard Business School explored in "Strategies for Learning from Failure" (HBR April 2011). Failure can lead to embarrassment and expose gaps in knowledge, which can undermine individuals' self-esteem and standing in an organization. After all, how often are managers promoted and teams rewarded for the early exposure of failures that lead a project to be killed—even though the early redeployment of precious resources benefits the company? This is especially true in organizations that have built a "zero tolerance for failure" or "error-free" (Six Sigma) environment.

Thomas Alva Edison understood all this. He organized his famous laboratories around the concept of rapid experimentation, locating machine shops for building models close to the rooms where experiments were conducted so that machinists could cooperate closely with researchers. The labs had libraries containing a vast number of volumes so that information could be found quickly; nearby storerooms with ample quantities of supplies; and a diverse workforce of craftsmen, scientists, and engineers. Edison wanted to make sure that when he or his people had an idea, it could be immediately turned into a working model or prototype. "The real measure of success is the number of experiments that can be crowded into 24 hours," he said.

---

**Advances in information technology,** such as computer-aided design, modeling, and simulation, have already allowed companies to make great strides in developing better products in less time and at a lower cost. Many companies, however, have not tapped the full potential of these tools, because their management thinking has not evolved as quickly as the technology: They still approach the highly variable information-generating work of product development as if it were like manufacturing. As advances in IT continue, the opportunity to improve the product-development process will become even greater. But so will the risks for companies that fail to recognize that product development is profoundly different from manufacturing.

**Originally published in May 2012.  Reprint** R1205E

# Innovation:
# The Classic Traps

*by Rosabeth Moss Kanter*

**INNOVATION IS BACK AT** the top of the corporate agenda. Never a fad, but always in or out of fashion, innovation gets rediscovered as a growth enabler every half-dozen years (about the length of a managerial generation). Too often, however, grand declarations about innovation are followed by mediocre execution that produces anemic results, and innovation groups are quietly disbanded in cost-cutting drives. Each generation embarks on the same enthusiastic quest for the next new thing and faces the same challenge of overcoming innovation stiflers. Over the past 25 years, I have conducted research and advised companies during at least four major waves of competitive challenges that led to widespread enthusiasm for innovation.

The first was the dawn of the global information age in the late 1970s and early 1980s, an era that introduced new industries and threatened to topple old ones. Entrepreneurs and foreign competitors imperiled established companies on their own turf. Information technology was beginning to evolve from the clunky mainframe to a consumer and desktop product, and companies such as Apple Computer made Silicon Valley garages the new base for product innovation in the United States. IBM emulated Apple's model by developing its PC in dingy surroundings in Boca Raton, Florida, freed from many corporate constraints. High-quality Japanese products, such as the Sony Walkman and Toyota cars, reflected not just good product design but also innovations in manufacturing processes that forced American giants to create their own programs to generate new ideas faster. "Total quality management" became a passion.

The second wave was the pressure to restructure during the takeover scare of the late 1980s. Buyout groups were attacking traditional companies, seeking to unlock the value of underutilized assets; "shareholder value" became a rallying cry. In Europe, restructuring was associated with the privatization of state-owned enterprises now exposed to the pressures of capital markets. Software was emerging as a major force behind innovation, and the strategic value of IT was touted, with American Airlines' Sabre reservations system widely cited as an example of a process innovation that succeeded as a separate business. Companies created new-venture departments to make sure they captured the value of their own ideas and inventions, rather than allowing a behemoth like Microsoft to arise outside the firm. Financial innovations were the rage: leveraged and management buyouts, derivatives and other forms of financial engineering, or financial supermarkets combining banks and nearly everything else. The restructuring era also favored products that could be instantly global: After defeating a hostile takeover bid in the late 1980s, Gillette boldly and successfully launched Sensor Excel shaving systems in the early 1990s, in identical form worldwide, with a single advertising message.

Third was the digital mania of the 1990s. The promise (and threat) of the World Wide Web drove many established companies to seek radical new business models. Brick-and-mortar companies were at risk for extinction; many rushed to create stand-alone Web ventures, often unconnected to the core business and sometimes in conflict with it. Eyes were on the capital markets rather than on customers, and companies got rich without profits or revenues. AOL bought Time Warner, put its name first, and proceeded to destroy value rather than create innovation.

The current wave of innovation began in a more sober mood, following the dot-com crash and belt-tightening of the global recession. Having recognized the limits of acquisitions and become skeptical about technology hype, companies refocused on organic growth. Surviving giants such as General Electric and IBM have

## Idea in Brief

Most companies fuel growth by creating new products and services. Yet too many firms repeat the same growth-sapping mistakes in their efforts to innovate.

For example, some companies adopt the wrong strategy: investing only in ideas they think will become blockbusters. Result? Small ideas that could have generated big profits get rejected. For years, Time, Inc. didn't develop new publications: managers wanted any start-up to succeed on the same scale as the enormously popular *People* magazine. Only after Time decided to gamble on a large number of new publications did revenues rise.

Other companies err on the side of process-strangling innovations by subjecting them to the strict performance criteria their existing businesses must follow. At AlliedSignal, new Internet-based products and services had to satisfy the same financial metrics as established businesses. Budgets contained no funds for investment—so managers working on innovations had to find their own funding. The consequences? Retrofitted versions of old ideas.

To avoid such traps, Kanter advocates applying lessons from past failures to your innovation efforts. For instance, augment potential "big bets" with promising midrange ideas and incremental innovations. And add flexibility to your innovation planning, budgeting, and reviews.

Your reward? Better odds that the new ideas percolating in your company today will score profitable successes in the market tomorrow.

---

adopted innovation as a corporate theme. GE, for instance, is committed to double-digit growth from within. For its part, IBM is seeking innovation by tackling difficult social problems that require—and showcase—its technology solutions. A good example is World Community Grid, a nonprofit IBM created that aggregates unused computer power from numerous partners to give AIDS researchers and other scientists the ability to work with unusually large data sets. This wave's central focus is on new products designed to offer users new features and functionality to meet emerging needs. Customers and consumer markets have returned to center stage, after having been temporarily crowded out by other obsessions. Companies are seeking new categories to enrich their existing businesses rather than grand new ventures that will take

## Idea in Practice

To innovate successfully, replace common mistakes with potent remedies.

### Strategy Mistakes

- Rejecting opportunities that at first glance appear too small.

- Assuming that only new products count—not new services or improved processes.

- Launching too many minor product extensions that confuse customers and increase internal complexity.

**Remedy: Widen your search and broaden your scope.** Support a few big bets at the top that represent clear directions for the future and receive the lion's share of investment. Also create a portfolio of promising midrange ideas. And fund a broad base of early stage ideas or incremental innovations.

### Process Mistakes

- Strangling innovation with the same tight planning, budgeting, and reviews applied to existing businesses.

- Rewarding managers for doing only what they committed to do—and discouraging them from making changes as circumstances warrant.

**Remedy: Add flexibility to planning and control systems.** For instance, reserve special funds for unexpected opportunities.

*Example:* After executives at the struggling UK television network BBC set aside funds in a corporate account to support innovation proposals, a new recruit used money originally allocated for a new BBC training film to make a pilot for *The Office*. The show became the BBC's biggest hit comedy in decades.

### Structure Mistakes

- Isolating fledgling and established enterprises in separate silos.

---

them into totally different realms. Signature innovations in this era include Apple's iPod and Procter & Gamble's Swiffer.

Each wave brought new concepts. For example, the rise of biotechnology, characterized by complicated licensing arrangements, helped legitimize the idea that established firms could outsource R&D and learn from entrepreneurial partners or that consumer products companies could turn to external idea shops, as well as their own labs, to invent new products. Approaches to

- Creating two classes of corporate citizens—those who have all the fun (innovators) and those who must make the money (mainstream business managers).

**Remedy: Tighten the human connections between innovators and others throughout your organization.** Convene frequent conversations between innovators and mainstream business managers to promote mutual learning and integration of new businesses into the organization. Create overlapping relationships—by having representatives from mainstream businesses rotate through innovation groups or innovation advisory boards. Identify people who lead informal networks that span innovation and mainstream groups, and encourage them to strengthen those connections.

### Skills Mistakes

- Allowing innovators to rotate out of teams so quickly that team chemistry can't gel.

- Assuming that innovation teams should be led by the best technical people.

**Remedy: Select innovation leaders with strong interpersonal skills.** They'll keep the innovation team intact, help innovation teams embrace collective goals, leverage one another's different strengths, and share hard-to-document knowledge while innovations are under development.

> *Example:* When Williams-Sonoma launched its ultimately successful e-commerce group, it put a manager in charge who wasn't a technology expert but who could assemble the right team. He chose a mixture of employees from other units who could be ambassadors to their former groups and new hires that brought diverse skills.

innovation also reflected changing economic conditions and geopolitical events. And, of course, innovation has covered a wide spectrum, including technologies, products, processes, and complete business ventures, each with its own requirements.

Still, despite changes to the environment and differences among types of innovation, each wave of enthusiasm has encountered similar dilemmas. Most of these stem from the tensions between protecting revenue streams from existing businesses critical to current success and supporting new concepts that may be crucial to future success. These tensions are exacerbated by the long-known phenomenon that important innovations often arise from outside an industry and beyond the established players, creating extra pressure for companies to find the next big concept quickly. Consequently, a large body of knowledge about innovation dilemmas has arisen.

Books such as Tom Peters and Bob Waterman's *In Search of Excellence,* my own *The Change Masters,* and Gifford Pinchot's *Intrapreneuring* supported the 1980s innovation wave by pointing to the importance of relieving potential innovators of bureaucratic constraints so they could run with their ideas. This was followed by a body of work documenting the difficulty of exploring the new while exploiting the old, reflected in Michael Tushman and Charles O'Reilly's call for more ambidextrous organizations in *Winning Through Innovation;* my work on managing the tensions between the powerful organizational mainstream and fragile new streams produced by innovation groups in *When Giants Learn to Dance;* and Clayton Christensen's more recent finding, in *The Innovator's Dilemma,* that listening to current customers can inhibit breakthrough innovation.

Yet despite all the research and literature, I still observe executives exhibiting the same lack of courage or knowledge that undercut previous waves of innovation. They declare that they want more innovation but then ask, "Who else is doing it?" They claim to seek new ideas but shoot down every one brought to them. And, repeatedly, companies make the same mistakes as their predecessors. For example, a 1983 HBR article by Harvard Business School professor Malcolm Salter, et al., "When Corporate Venture Capital Doesn't Work," provided warnings that companies failed to heed about exactly the same dilemmas they face today: With a few notable exceptions, such as Intel and Reuters, companies' venture-capital departments rarely create significant value for the core business.

It's inevitable that historical memory will fade—but not inevitable that we lose the lessons. Here's a chance to collect some of what is known about innovation traps and how to avoid them.

## Strategy Mistakes: Hurdles Too High, Scope Too Narrow

The potential for premium prices and high margins lures executives to seek blockbuster innovations—the next iPod, Viagra, or Toyota Production System. Along the way, they expend enormous resources, though big hits are rare and unpredictable. Meanwhile, in seeking the killer app, managers may reject opportunities that at first glance appear too small, and people who aren't involved in the big projects may feel marginalized.

For years, large consumer products companies typically screened out ideas that couldn't result in revenues of several hundred million dollars within two years. This screen discouraged investments in ideas that couldn't be tested and measured using conventional market research, or that weren't grounded in experience, in favor of ideas that were close to current practice and hardly innovative. In the 1980s and 1990s, Pillsbury, Quaker Oats, and even Procter & Gamble (an innovation powerhouse today) were vulnerable to smaller companies that could quickly roll out new products, thus eroding the giants' market share. P&G, for example, lamented not having introduced a new toilet bowl cleaner before a competitor did, despite P&G labs' having developed similar technology. The rival, of course, gained dominant market share by being a first mover. Likewise, Pillsbury and Quaker lagged the competition in bringing new concepts to market and, as underperformers, were eventually acquired.

Time Incorporated, the magazine wing of Time Warner, for a long time was slow to develop new publications because managers wanted any start-up to have the potential to grow into another *People* or *Sports Illustrated,* two of the company's legendary successes. During the period before Don Logan took the helm in 1992, almost no new magazines were launched. After Logan brought a different innovation strategy to the magazine group, Time developed (or bought) about 100 magazines, which dramatically increased the company's revenues, cash flow, and profits. Not every offering was a blockbuster, but Time had learned what successful innovators know: To get more successes, you have to be willing to risk more failures.

# The Lessons of Innovation

INNOVATION GOES IN OR OUT of fashion as a strategic driver of corporate growth, but with every wave of enthusiasm, executives make the same mistakes. Most of the time, they stumble in their R&D efforts because they are engaged in a difficult balancing act: They need to protect existing revenue streams while coaxing along new ones. But "corporate entrepreneurship" doesn't have to be an oxymoron. Innovation can flourish if executives heed business lessons from the past.

## Strategy Lessons

- Not every innovation idea has to be a blockbuster. Sufficient numbers of small or incremental innovations can lead to big profits.

- Don't just focus on new product development: Transformative ideas can come from any function—for instance, marketing, production, finance, or distribution.

- Successful innovators use an "innovation pyramid," with several big bets at the top that get most of the investment; a portfolio of promising midrange ideas in test stage; and a broad base of early stage ideas or incremental innovations. Ideas and influence can flow up or down the pyramid.

## Process Lessons

- Tight controls strangle innovation. The planning, budgeting, and reviews applied to existing businesses will squeeze the life out of an innovation effort.

A related mistake is to act as if only products count, even though transformative new ideas can come from a range of functions, such as production and marketing. For instance, a fabric company that made complicated woven materials had a long-standing problem: yarn breakage during production, which was reflected in the cost of the company's products and represented a competitive disadvantage. But the top team at the fabric maker continued to talk about the company's search for really big product innovations, such as totally new materials. A new executive, who believed in opening the search for innovation to all employees, joined the company. After a meeting discussing the need for change, a veteran factory worker, who had joined as a young immigrant and still spoke with a heavy

- Companies should expect deviations from plan: If employees are rewarded simply for doing what they committed to do, rather than acting as circumstances would suggest, their employers will stifle and drive out innovation.

**Structure Lessons**

- While loosening formal controls, companies should tighten interpersonal connections between innovation efforts and the rest of the business.

- Game-changing innovations often cut across established channels or combine elements of existing capacity in new ways.

- If companies create two classes of corporate citizens—supplying the innovators with more perks, privileges, and prestige—those in the existing business will make every effort to crush the innovation.

**Skills Lessons**

- Even the most technical of innovations requires strong leaders with great relationship and communication skills.

- Members of successful innovation teams stick together through the development of an idea, even if the company's approach to career timing requires faster job rotation.

- Because innovations need connectors—people who know how to find partners in the mainstream business or outside world—they flourish in cultures that encourage collaboration.

accent, tentatively approached the new executive with an idea for ending the breakage. The company tried it, and it worked. When asked how long he had had that idea, the worker replied, "Thirty-two years."

Similarly, because managers at Quaker Oats in the 1990s were too busy tweaking product formulas in minor ways, the company missed numerous opportunities in other arenas, such as distribution—for instance, taking advantage of the smaller, health-oriented outlets used by its Snapple beverage acquisition. And in a packaging coup, Ocean Spray, the cranberry juice company, stole a march on America's largest juice purveyors (then including P&G and Coca-Cola) by getting an 18-month exclusive license for the introduction of Tetra Pak's paper bottles to the U.S. market. Ocean Spray boasted a more eclectic innovation strategy than that of its rivals, including idea forums to explore innovations in any domain and open to any employee. Paper bottles were an instant hit with children (and parents packing their lunches), and Ocean Spray's market share shot way up.

Early in its history, the U.S. auto industry gained a breakthrough innovation from its financial function: Consumer financing opened mass markets for products that previously only the affluent could afford. One Intel breakthrough was in marketing: It treated computer chips like potato chips. As a technology company, Intel could have left innovation to its R&D folks. But by marketing a component directly to consumers, Intel gained enormous power with computer manufacturers, which had little choice but to put an Intel Inside label on every machine.

Similarly, Cemex, the global cement company based in Mexico, has used widespread brainstorming to generate innovations that create other sources of value for a product that could easily become a commodity. Those innovations include branded, bagged cement and technology-enabled delivery methods to get cement to customers as fast as if it were a pizza. And while P&G is getting attention for its product innovations, such as the Swiffer and Crest Whitestrips, its innovations in new media, such as interactive Web sites for the soap operas it sponsors, may prove even more valuable for the company's future.

When a company is both too product centric and too revenue impatient, an additional problem can arise. The organization's innovation energy can dissipate across a raft of tiny me-too projects chasing immediate revenue. Perversely, such projects may raise costs in the long run. While a failure to encourage small wins can mean missed opportunities, too many trivial projects are like seeds sown on stony ground—they might sprout, but they do not take root and grow into anything useful. If new ideas take the form not of distinctive innovations but of modest product variations, the resulting proliferation can dilute the brand, confuse customers, and increase internal complexity—such as offering a dozen sizes and flavors of crackers rather than a new and different snack food, a problem Kraft currently faces.

## Process Mistakes: Controls Too Tight

A second set of classic mistakes lies in process; specifically, the impulse to strangle innovation with tight controls—the same planning, budgeting, and reviews applied to existing businesses. The inherent uncertainty of the innovation process makes sidetracks or unexpected turns inevitable. The reason upstart Ocean Spray could grab the paper-bottle opportunity from large U.S. juice makers is that the big companies' funds had already been allocated for the year, and they wanted committees to study the packaging option before making commitments that would deviate from their plans.

AlliedSignal (now Honeywell) in 2000 sought new Internet-based products and services using established strategic-planning and budgeting processes through existing business units. The CEO asked the divisions to bring their best ideas for Internet-related innovations to the quarterly budget reviews. Although designated as a priority, these innovation projects were subjected to the same financial metrics the established businesses were. Budgets contained no additional funds for investment; managers working on innovations had to find their own sources of funding through savings or internal transfers. What emerged were often retrofitted versions of ideas that had been in the pipeline anyway.

Performance reviews, and their associated metrics, are another danger zone for innovations. Established companies don't just want plans; they want managers to stick to those plans. They often reward people for doing what they committed to do and discourage them from making changes as circumstances warrant. At a large defense contractor, for instance, people got low marks for not delivering exactly what they had promised, even if they delivered something better—which led people to underpromise, eventually reducing employees' aspirations and driving out innovation.

In the early 1990s, Bank of Boston (now part of Bank of America) set up an innovative unit called First Community Bank (FCB), the first comprehensive banking initiative to focus on inner-city markets. FCB struggled to convince mainstream managers in Bank of Boston's retail-banking group that the usual performance metrics, such as transaction time and profitability per customer, were not appropriate for this market—which required customer education, among other things—or for a new venture that still needed investment. Mainstream managers argued that "underperforming" branches should be closed. In order to save the innovation, FCB leaders had to invent their own metrics, based on customer satisfaction and loyalty, and find creative ways to show results by clusters of branches. The venture later proved both profitable and important to the parent bank as it embarked on a series of acquisitions.

## Structure Mistakes: Connections Too Loose, Separations Too Sharp

While holding fledgling enterprises to the same processes as established businesses is dangerous, companies must be careful how they structure the two entities, to avoid a clash of cultures or conflicting agendas.

The more dramatic approach is to create a unit apart from the mainstream business, which must still serve its embedded base. This was the logic behind the launch of Saturn as an autonomous subsidiary of General Motors. GM's rules were suspended, and the Saturn team was encouraged to innovate in every aspect of vehicle design, production, marketing, sales, and customer service. The hope was that the best ideas would be incorporated back at the parent company, but instead, after a successful launch, Saturn was reintegrated into GM, and many of its innovations disappeared.

In the time it took for Saturn to hit its stride, Toyota—which favored continuous improvement over blockbusters or greenfield initiatives like Saturn—was still ahead of GM in quality, customer satisfaction, and market share growth. Similarly, U.S. charter schools were freed from the rules of public school systems so they could innovate and thus serve as models for improved education. They've employed many innovative practices, including longer school days and focused curricula, but there is little evidence that charter schools have influenced changes in the rest of their school districts.

The problem in both cases can be attributed to poor connections between the greenfield and the mainstream. Indeed, when people operate in silos, companies may miss innovation opportunities altogether. Game-changing innovations often cut across established channels or combine elements of existing capacity in new ways. CBS was once the world's largest broadcaster and owned the world's largest record company, yet it failed to invent music video, losing this opportunity to MTV. In the late 1990s, Gillette had a toothbrush unit (Oral B), an appliance unit (Braun), and a battery unit (Duracell), but lagged in introducing a battery-powered toothbrush.

The likelihood that companies will miss or stifle innovations increases when the potential innovations involve expertise from different industries or knowledge of different technologies. Managers at established organizations may both fail to understand the nature of a new idea and feel threatened by it.

AT&T Worldnet, the Internet access venture of the venerable long-distance telephone company, faced this lethal mix in the mid-1990s. Managers in the traditional consumer services and business services units participated in a series of debates over whether to manage Worldnet as a distinct business unit, with its own P&L, or to include it in the existing business units focused primarily on the consumer sector. While consumer services managers were reluctant to let go of anything, they eventually agreed to a carve-out intended to protect the embryonic venture from being crushed by the bureaucracy and to keep it from being measured against more-mature businesses that were generating significant cash flow rather than requiring investment. They weren't all that concerned, because they believed an Internet service provider would never generate significant revenue and profitability.

But as Worldnet gained momentum, it attracted more attention. The people in consumer services began to view the innovation's possible expansion to provide voice over Internet protocol (VoIP) services as a threat that could cannibalize existing business. Consumer services managers grabbed control of Worldnet and proceeded to starve it. They used it as a platform to sell core land-based long-distance services and started applying the same metrics to the Internet business that were used for consumer long-distance. Pricing was an immediate problem. Worldnet's services had been priced low to fuel growth, to get the scale and network effects of a large group of subscribers, but the mainstream unit did not want to incur losses on any line of business. So it raised prices, and Worldnet's growth stalled. Consumer services managers could then treat Worldnet as a trivial, slow-growing business, not worthy of large investment. They did not allocate sufficient resources to develop Internet access and VoIP technology, restraining important telecom innovations in which AT&T could have been the pioneer.

Cultural clashes exacerbated tensions at AT&T. Mainstream managers had long tenures in the Bell system. The Internet group, however, hired external tech professionals who spoke the language of computers, not telephony.

Even when a new venture is launched within an existing business, culture clashes become class warfare if there are two classes of corporate citizens—those who have all the fun and those who make all the money. The designated innovators, whether an R&D group or a new-venture unit, are identified as creators of the future. They are free of rules or revenue demands and are allowed to play with ideas that don't yet work. Their colleagues are expected to follow rules, meet demands, and make money while feeling like grinds and sometimes being told they are dinosaurs whose business models will soon be obsolete.

In the early 2000s, Arrow Electronics' attempt at an Internet venture, Arrow.com, was given space in the same facility as the traditional sales force. The similarities stopped there. The Internet group was composed of new hires, often young, from a different background, who dressed in a completely different style. It spent money on cushy furniture, including a big expenditure on a new kitchen—justified, it was said, because the Arrow.com team worked 24/7. The traditional sales force, already anxious about the threat Internet-enabled sales posed to its commissions and now aware of its dingier offices, became overtly angry. Relations between the groups grew so acrimonious that a brick wall was erected to separate the two sides of the building. Both teams wasted time battling, endangering customer relationships when the two groups fought over the same customers—after all, Arrow.com was just another distribution channel. The CEO had to intervene and find structures to connect them.

## Skills Mistakes: Leadership Too Weak, Communication Too Poor

Undervaluing and underinvesting in the human side of innovation is another common mistake. Top managers frequently put the best technical people in charge, not the best leaders. These technically oriented managers, in turn, mistakenly assume that ideas will speak for themselves if they are any good, so they neglect external communication. Or they emphasize tasks over relationships, missing opportunities to enhance the team chemistry necessary to turn undeveloped concepts into useful innovations.

Groups that are convened without attention to interpersonal skills find it difficult to embrace collective goals, take advantage of the different strengths various members bring, or communicate well enough to share the tacit knowledge that is still unformed and hard to document while an innovation is under development. It takes time to build the trust and interplay among team members that will spark great ideas. MIT researchers have found that for R&D team members to be truly productive, they have to have been on board for at least two years. At one point, Pillsbury realized that the average length of time the company took to go from new product idea to successful commercialization was 24 to 26 months, but the average length of time people spent on product teams was 18 months. No wonder the company was falling behind in innovation.

Changes in team composition that result from companies' preferences for the frequency with which individuals make career moves can make it hard for new ventures to deal with difficult challenges, prompting them to settle for quick, easy, conventional solutions. At Honeywell in the 1980s, leaders of new-venture teams were often promoted out of them before the work had been completed. Because promotions were take-it-or-leave-it offers and pay was tied to size of assets controlled (small by definition in new ventures) rather than difficulty of task, even dedicated innovators saw the virtues of leaving their projects midstream. Honeywell was undermining its own innovation efforts. An executive review of why new ventures failed uncovered this problem, but a technology bias made it hard for old-school managers of that era to increase their appreciation for the value of team bonding and continuity.

Innovation efforts also bog down when communication and relationship building outside the team are neglected. When Gap Incorporated was struggling in the late 1990s, the company mounted several cross-unit projects to find innovations in products, retail concepts, and operations. Some of the project teams quickly became closed environments, and members cut themselves off from their former peers. By failing to tap others' ideas, they produced lackluster recommendations; and by failing to keep peers informed, they missed getting buy-in for even their weak proposals.

Innovators cannot work in isolation if they want their concepts to catch on. They must build coalitions of supporters who will provide air cover for the project, speak up for them in meetings they don't attend, or sponsor the embryonic innovation as it moves into the next stages of diffusion and use. To establish the foundation for successful reception of an innovation, groups must be able to present the radical so it can be understood in familiar terms and to cushion disruptive innovations with assurances that the disruption will be manageable. When technical experts mystify their audiences rather than enlighten them, they lose support—and "no" is always an easier answer than "yes." Groups that work in secret and then present their ideas fullblown at the end face unexpected objections that sometimes kill the project.

Such inattention to relationships and communication with mainstream business managers doomed the launch of Timberland's promising TravelGear line. Developed by an R&D group called the Invention Factory, which was independent of the company's mainstream businesses, TravelGear allowed a user to travel with a single pair of shoes, adding or subtracting components suitable for a range of outdoor activities. The concept won a design award from *Business-Week* in 2005. But some existing business teams had not been included in the Invention Factory's developments, and the traditional sales force refused to sell TravelGear products.

By contrast, Dr. Craig Feied's success in developing a state-of-the-art digital network for Washington Hospital Center and its parent, MedStar Health, was a testimony to investment in the human dimension. A small group of programmers designed a user-friendly information system in the emergency department, not the IT department, so they were already close to users. Dr. Feied and his partner, Dr. Mark Smith, made a point of sitting on numerous hospital committees so they would have a wide base of relationships. Their investment in people and their contributions toward shared hospital goals had a positive effect: Feied and Smith's actions helped create good word of mouth and support among other departments for their information system (now called Azyxxi), which resulted in saved time and lives.

The climate for relationships within an innovation group is shaped by the climate outside it. Having a negative instead of a positive culture can cost a company real money. During Seagate Technology's troubled period in the mid-to-late 1990s, the company, a large manufacturer of disk drives for personal computers, had seven different design centers working on innovation, yet it had the lowest R&D productivity in the industry because the centers competed rather than cooperated. Attempts to bring them together merely led people to advocate for their own groups rather than find common ground. Not only did Seagate's engineers and managers lack positive norms for group interaction, but they had the opposite in place: People who yelled in executive meetings received "Dog's Head" awards for the worst conduct. Lack of product and process innovation was reflected in loss of market share, disgruntled customers, and declining sales. Seagate, with its dwindling PC sales and fading customer base, was threatening to become a commodity producer in a changing technology environment.

Under a new CEO and COO, Steve Luczo and Bill Watkins, who operated as partners, Seagate developed new norms for how people should treat one another, starting with the executive group. Their raised consciousness led to a systemic process for forming and running "core teams" (cross-functional innovation groups), and Seagate employees were trained in common methodologies for team building, both in conventional training programs and through participation in difficult outdoor activities in New Zealand and other remote locations. To lead core teams, Seagate promoted people who were known for strong relationship skills above others with greater technical skills. Unlike the antagonistic committees convened during the years of decline, the core teams created dramatic process and product innovations that brought the company back to market leadership. The new Seagate was able to create innovations embedded in a wide range of new electronic devices, such as iPods and cell phones.

## Innovation Remedies

The quest for breakthrough ideas, products, and services can get derailed in any or all of the ways described earlier. Fortunately, however, history also shows how innovation succeeds. "Corporate entrepreneurship" need not be an oxymoron. Here are four ways to win.

### Strategy remedy: Widen the search, broaden the scope

Companies can develop an innovation strategy that works at the three levels of what I call the "innovation pyramid": a few big bets at the top that represent clear directions for the future and receive the lion's share of investment; a portfolio of promising midrange ideas pursued by designated teams that develop and test them; and a broad base of early stage ideas or incremental innovations permitting continuous improvement. Influence flows down the pyramid, as the big bets encourage small wins heading in the same direction, but it also can flow up, because big innovations sometimes begin life as small bits of tinkering—as in the famously accidental development of 3M's Post-it Notes.

Thinking of innovation in terms of this pyramid gives senior managers a tool for assessing current efforts, making adjustments as ideas prove their value and require further support, and ensuring that there is activity at all levels. A culture of innovation grows because everyone can play. While dedicated groups pursue the big projects and temporary teams develop midrange ideas, everyone else in the company can be invited to contribute ideas. Every employee can be a potential idea scout and project initiator, as IBM is demonstrating. This past July, the company held a three-day InnovationJam on the Web, during which about 140,000 employees and clients—representing 104 countries—contributed about 37,000 ideas and ranked them, giving the company an enormous pool of raw ideas, some of them big, most of them small. Indeed, an organization is more likely to get bigger ideas if it has a wide funnel into which numerous small ideas can be poured. One of the secrets of success for companies that demonstrate high rates of innovation is that they simply try more things.

Gillette adopted the pyramid model as part of its push to accelerate innovation in 2003 and 2004. The result was a stream of innovations in every function and business unit that raised revenues and profits. They included new products such as a battery-powered toothbrush; new concepts in the R&D pipeline, such as the 2006 five-blade, battery-powered Fusion shaving system; innovative marketing campaigns that neutralized the competition, such as the campaign for the Mach3Turbo, which outshone Schick's introduction of its Quattro razor; and new technology in HR. At the first Gillette innovation fair in March 2004, every unit showcased its best ideas of the year in a creative way. The legal department promoted its novel online ethics course with a joke: distributing "get out of jail free" cards like those in *Monopoly*. Having the legal department embrace innovation was a plus for a company in which innovators needed speedy service to file patent applications or help to clear regulatory hurdles.

An innovation strategy that includes incremental innovations and continuous improvement can help to liberate minds throughout the company, making people more receptive to change when big breakthroughs occur.

### Process remedy: Add flexibility to planning and control systems

One way to encourage innovation to flourish outside the normal planning cycles is to reserve pools of special funds for unexpected opportunities. That way, promising ideas do not have to wait for the next budget cycle, and innovators do not have to beg for funds from mainstream managers who are measured on current revenues and profits. In the mid-to-late 1990s, autocratic management and rigid controls caused the BBC to slip in program innovation and, consequently, audience share. Budgets were tight, and, once they were set, expenditures were confined to predetermined categories. In 2000, a new CEO and his CFO relaxed the rules and began setting aside funds in a corporate account to support proposals for innovation, making it clear that bureaucratic rules should not stand in the way of creative ideas. The BBC's biggest hit comedy in decades, *The Office,* was an accident, made possible when a new recruit took the initiative to use money originally allocated for a BBC training film to make the pilot.

IBM is building such flexibility directly into its infrastructure. The company established a $100 million innovation fund to support the best ideas arising from its InnovationJam, independent of the normal planning and budgeting processes, to allow bottom-up ideas to flourish. "No one has ever before brought together such a global and diverse set of business thought leaders on this scale to discuss the most pressing issues and opportunities of our age," says Nick Donofrio, IBM's executive vice president of innovation and technology. "We have companies literally knocking at the door and saying, 'Give us your best and brightest ideas, and let's work together to make them a reality.' It's a golden opportunity to create entirely new markets and partnerships."

Besides needing different funding models and development partnerships, the innovation process requires exemption from some corporate requirements; after all, there are numerous differences between established businesses and new ventures. For example, the knowledge that innovations could move forward through rapid prototyping—learning from a series of fast trials—might mean that certain milestones triggering review and additional funding would occur faster than they would for established businesses, following the rhythm of the project rather than a fixed quarterly or annual calendar. For other kinds of projects, greater patience might be required— for instance, when an innovation group encounters unexpected obstacles and needs to rethink its model. The key is flexible, customized treatment.

### Structure remedy: Facilitate close connections
### between innovators and mainstream businesses

While loosening the formal controls that would otherwise stifle innovations, companies should tighten the human connections between those pursuing innovation efforts and others throughout the rest of the business. Productive conversations should take place regularly between innovators and mainstream business managers. Innovation teams should be charged with external communication as part of their responsibility, but senior leaders should also convene discussions to encourage mutual respect rather than tensions and antagonism. Such conversations should be aimed at mutual learning, to minimize cannibalization and to maximize effective reintegration of innovations that become new businesses. In addition to formal meetings, companies can facilitate informal conversations—as Steelcase did by building a design center that would force people to bump into one another—or identify the people who lead informal cross-unit networks and encourage their efforts at making connections.

Innovation groups can be told at the outset that they have a responsibility to serve the mainstream while also seeking bigger innovations to start new businesses. This can be built into their charters and reinforced by overlapping relationships—whether it involves representatives from mainstream businesses rotating through innovation groups or advisory boards overseeing innovation efforts. After its first great idea flopped, Timberland's Invention Factory learned to work closely with mainstream teams to meet their needs for immediate innovations, such as recreational shoes lined with SmartWool, and to seek game-changing breakthroughs. Turner Broadcasting's new-products group mixes project types: stand-alone developments, enhancements for current channels, external partnerships, and venture capital investments. PNC Financial Services Group recently established a new-products group to oversee mainstream developments, such as pricing and product enhancements, as well as growth engines in new capabilities, such as technology-enabled services and back-office services for investment funds. The company's sales of emerging products were up 21% in 2005, accounting for 46% of all sales.

Flexible organizational structures, in which teams across functions or disciplines organize around solutions, can facilitate good connections. Media conglomerate Publicis has "holistic communication" teams, which combine people across its ad agencies (Saatchi & Saatchi, Leo Burnett, Publicis Worldwide, and so on) and technology groups to focus on customers and brands. Novartis has organized around diseases, with R&D more closely connected to markets and customers; this has helped the company introduce pathbreaking innovations faster, such as its cancer drug Gleevec. The success of Seagate's companywide Factory of the Future team at introducing seemingly miraculous process innovations led to widespread use of its core-teams model.

Would-be innovators at AlliedSignal discovered that tackling promising opportunities required outreach across silos. For example, the aerospace division was organized into groups that were dedicated to large commercial airlines, small commercial airlines, and general aviation (private and charter planes), but the best new idea involved differentiating customers by whether they performed their own maintenance or contracted it to others. The division needed to create new connections across previously divided territories in order to begin the innovation process.

The success of Williams-Sonoma as a multichannel retailer innovating in e-commerce can be attributed to the ways its Web pioneers connected their developments to the rest of the company. From the very beginning, CEO Howard Lester refused to consider Internet ventures that were independent of other company operations. The first main Web development was a bridal registry to create new functionality for the mainstream business. When this pilot project proved its value, an e-commerce department was launched and housed in its own building. But rather than standing apart and pursuing its own direction, that department sought to enhance existing channels, not compete with them. It measured its success not only according to e-commerce sales but also according to incremental sales through other channels that the Web had facilitated. To further its close connections with the mainstream business, the department offered free training to the rest of the company.

### Skills remedy: Select for leadership and interpersonal skills, and surround innovators with a supportive culture of collaboration

Companies that cultivate leadership skills are more likely to net successful innovations. One reason Williams-Sonoma could succeed in e-commerce quickly and profitably was its careful attention to the human dimension. Shelley Nandkeolyar, the first manager of Williams-Sonoma's e-commerce group, was not the most knowledgeable about the technology, but he was a leader who could assemble the right team. He valued relationships, so he chose a mixture of current employees from other units, who could be ambassadors to their former groups, and new hires that brought new skills. He added cross-company teams to advise and link to the e-commerce team. He invented an integrator role to better connect operations groups and chose Patricia Skerritt, known for being relationship oriented, to fill it.

Similarly, Gail Snowden was able to steer Bank of Boston's First Community Bank through the minefields of middle-manager antagonism toward a successful innovation that produced other innovations (new products and services) because of her leadership skills, not her banking skills. She built a close-knit team of talented people who bonded with one another and felt passion for the mission. Soon her group became one of the parent bank's most desirable places to work. She developed strong relationships with senior executives who helped her deal with tensions in the middle, and she communicated well and often about why her unit needed to be different. Her creativity, vision, teamwork, and persistence helped this group succeed and become a national role model, while other banks' efforts faltered.

IBM's big innovations, such as demonstrating grid computing through World Community Grid, are possible only because the company's culture encourages people to collaborate. CEO Sam

Palmisano has engaged hundreds of thousands of IBMers in a Web-based discussion of company values, and Nick Donofrio, IBM's executive vice president for innovation and technology, works to make 90,000 technical people around the world feel part of one innovation-seeking community. The corporate champion of World Community Grid, IBM vice president Stanley Litow, sought out partners in its business units and geographies to move the innovation forward.

Established companies can avoid falling into the classic traps that stifle innovation by widening the search for new ideas, loosening overly tight controls and rigid structures, forging better connections between innovators and mainstream operations, and cultivating communication and collaboration skills.

Innovation involves ideas that create the future. But the quest for innovation is doomed unless the managers who seek it take time to learn from the past. Getting the balance right between exploiting (getting the highest returns from current activities) and exploring (seeking the new) requires organizational flexibility and a great deal of attention to relationships. It always has, and it always will.

**Originally published in November 2006. Reprint R0611C**

# Discovery-Driven Planning

*by Rita Gunther McGrath*
*and Ian C. MacMillan*

**BUSINESS LORE IS FULL** of stories about smart companies that incur huge losses when they enter unknown territory—new alliances, new markets, new products, new technologies. The Walt Disney Company's 1992 foray into Europe with its theme park had accumulated losses of more than $1 billion by 1994. Zapmail, a fax product, cost Federal Express Corporation $600 million before it was dropped. Polaroid lost $200 million when it ventured into instant movies. Why do such efforts often defeat even experienced, smart companies? One obvious answer is that strategic ventures are inherently risky: The probability of failure simply comes with the territory. But many failures could be prevented or their cost contained if senior managers approached innovative ventures with the right planning and control tools.

Discovery-driven planning is a practical tool that acknowledges the difference between planning for a new venture and planning for a more conventional line of business. Conventional planning operates on the premise that managers can extrapolate future results from a well-understood and predictable platform of past experience. One expects predictions to be accurate because they are based on solid knowledge rather than on assumptions. In platform-based planning, a venture's deviations from plan are a bad thing.

The platform-based approach may make sense for ongoing businesses, but it is sheer folly when applied to new ventures. By definition, new ventures call for a company to envision what is unknown, uncertain, and not yet obvious to the competition. The safe, reliable, predictable knowledge of the well-understood business has not yet emerged. Instead, managers must make do with assumptions about the possible futures on which new businesses are based. New ventures are undertaken with a high ratio of assumption to knowledge. With ongoing businesses, one expects the ratio to be the exact opposite. Because assumptions about the unknown generally turn out to be wrong, new ventures inevitably experience deviations—often huge ones—from their original planned targets. Indeed, new ventures frequently require fundamental redirection.

Rather than trying to force startups into the planning methodologies for existing predictable and well-understood businesses, discovery-driven planning acknowledges that at the start of a new venture, little is known and much is assumed. When platform-based planning is used, assumptions underlying a plan are treated as facts—givens to be baked into the plan—rather than as best-guess estimates to be tested and questioned. Companies then forge ahead on the basis of those buried assumptions. In contrast, discovery-driven planning systematically converts assumptions into knowledge as a strategic venture unfolds. When new data are uncovered, they are incorporated into the evolving plan. The real potential of the venture is discovered as it develops— hence the term discovery-driven planning. The approach imposes disciplines different from, but no less precise than, the disciplines used in conventional planning.

## Euro Disney and the Platform-Based Approach

Even the best companies can run into serious trouble if they don't recognize the assumptions buried in their plans. The Walt Disney Company, a 49% owner of Euro Disney (now called Disneyland Paris), is known as an astute manager of theme parks. Its success has not been confined to the United States: Tokyo Disneyland has been a financial and public relations success almost from its opening in 1983. Euro Disney is another story, however. By 1993, attendance approached 1 million visitors each month, making the park Europe's most popular paid tourist destination. Then why did it lose so much money?

# Idea in Brief

You're weighing a major strategic venture—a first-time alliance, a new market, an innovative product. Beware: business history is littered with stories about smart companies that hemorrhaged multiple millions from ventures gone bad.

Why such massive losses? Too many firms use conventional planning to manage their ventures, say McGrath and MacMillan. They make predictions about a venture's potential based on their established businesses. And they treat the assumptions underlying those predictions—"The product will sell itself," "We'll have no competitors"—as facts. By the time they realize a key assumption was flawed, it's too late to stanch the bleeding.

How to avoid this scenario? As your venture unfolds, use a disciplined process to systematically uncover, test, and (if necessary) revise the assumptions behind your venture's plan. You'll expose the make-or-break uncertainties common to ventures. And you'll address those uncertainties at the lowest possible cost—so you don't set your venture on the path to ruin.

In planning Euro Disney in 1986, Disney made projections that drew on its experience from its other parks. The company expected half of the revenue to come from admissions, the other half from hotels, food, and merchandise. Although by 1993, Euro Disney had succeeded in reaching its target of 11 million admissions, to do so it had been forced to drop adult ticket prices drastically. The average spending per visit was far below plan and added to the red ink.

The point is not to play Monday-morning quarterback with Disney's experience but to demonstrate an approach that could have revealed flawed assumptions and mitigated the resulting losses. The discipline of systematically identifying key assumptions would have highlighted the business plan's vulnerabilities. Let us look at each source of revenue in turn.

### Admissions price

In Japan and the United States, Disney found its price by raising it over time, letting early visitors go back home and talk up the park to their neighbors. But the planners of Euro Disney assumed that they could hit their target number of visitors even if they started out with

## Idea in Practice

McGrath and MacMillan suggest this five-step process for successful venture planning:

### 1. Bake Profitability into Your Venture's Plan

Instead of estimating the venture's revenues and then assuming profits will come, create a "reverse income statement" for the project: Determine the profit required to make the venture worthwhile—it should be at least 10%. Then calculate the revenues needed to deliver that profit.

### 2. Calculate Allowable Costs

Lay out all the activities required to produce, sell, service, and deliver the new product or service to customers. Together, these activities comprise the venture's **allowable costs**. Ask, "If we subtract allowable costs from required revenues, will the venture deliver significant returns?" If not, it may not be worth the risk.

### 3. Identify Your Assumptions

If you still think the venture *is* worth the risk, work with other managers on the venture team to list all the assumptions behind your profit, revenue, and allowable costs calculations. Use disagreement over assumptions to trigger discussion, and be open to adjusting your list.

---

an admission price of more than $40 per adult. A major recession in Europe and the determination of the French government to keep the franc strong exacerbated the problem and led to low attendance. Although companies cannot control macroeconomic events, they can highlight and test their pricing assumptions. Euro Disney's prices were very high compared with those of other theme attractions in Europe, such as the aqua palaces, which charged low entry fees and allowed visitors to build their own menus by paying for each attraction individually. By 1993, Euro Disney not only had been forced to make a sharp price reduction to secure its target visitors, it had also lost the benefits of early-stage word of mouth. The talking-up phenomenon is especially important in Europe, as Disney could have gauged from the way word of mouth had benefited Club Med.

### Hotel accommodations

Based on its experience in other markets, Disney assumed that people would stay an average of four days in the park's five hotels.

*Example:* A company has determined that it needs to sell 250 million units of a proposed new product at a particular price to generate the revenue required to meet the venture's profit goal. It decides how many orders it'll need to sell the 250 million units, how many sales calls it'll take to secure those orders, how many salespeople will be required to make those calls, and how much this will cost in sales-force compensation.

### 4. Determine If the Venture Still Makes Sense

Check your assumptions against your reverse income statement for the venture. Can you still make the required profit, given your latest estimates of revenues and allowable costs? If not, the venture should be scrapped.

### 5. Test Assumptions at Milestones

If you've decided to move ahead with the venture, use milestone events to test—and, if necessary, further update—your assumptions. Postpone major commitments of resources until evidence from a previous milestone signals that taking the next step is justified.

The average stay in 1993 was only two days. Had the assumption been highlighted, it might have been challenged: Since Euro Disney opened with only 15 rides, compared with 45 at Disney World, people could do them all in a single day.

### Food

Park visitors in the United States and Japan "graze" all day. At Euro Disney, the buried assumption was that Europeans would do the same. Euro Disney's restaurants, therefore, were designed for all-day streams of grazers. When floods of visitors tried to follow the European custom of dining at noon, Disney was unable to seat them. Angry visitors left the park to eat, and they conveyed their anger to their friends and neighbors back home.

### Merchandise

Although Disney did forecast lower sales per visitor in Europe than in the United States and Japan, the company assumed that Europeans would buy a similar mix of cloth goods and print items. Instead, Euro Disney fell short of plan when visitors bought a far smaller proportion of high-margin items such as T-shirts and hats than expected. Disney could have tested the buried assumption before forecasting sales: Disney's retail stores in European cities sell many fewer of the high-margin cloth items and far more of the low-margin print items.

Disney is not alone. Other companies have paid a significant price for pursuing platform-based ventures built on implicit assumptions that turn out to be faulty. Such ventures are usually undertaken without careful up-front identification and validation of those assumptions, which often are unconscious. We have repeatedly observed that the following four planning errors are characteristic of this approach.

*Companies don't have hard data but, once a few key decisions are made, proceed as though their assumptions were facts.* Euro Disney's implicit assumptions regarding the way visitors would use hotels and restaurants are good examples.

*Companies have all the hard data they need to check assumptions but fail to see the implications.* After making assumptions based on a subset of the available data, they proceed without ever testing those assumptions. Federal Express based Zapmail on the assumption that there would be a substantial demand for four-hour delivery of documents faxed from FedEx center to FedEx center. What went unchallenged was the implicit assumption that customers would not be able to afford their own fax machines before long. If that assumption had been unearthed, FedEx would have been more likely to take into account the plunging prices and increasing sales of fax machines for the office and, later, for the home.

*Companies possess all the data necessary to determine that a real opportunity exists but make implicit and inappropriate assumptions about their ability to implement their plan.* Exxon lost $200 million on its office automation business by implicitly assuming that it could build a direct sales and service support capability to compete head-to-head with IBM and Xerox.

*Companies start off with the right data, but they implicitly assume a static environment and thus fail to notice until too late that a key*

---

### Some dangerous implicit assumptions

1. Customers will buy our product because we think it's a good product.
2. Customers will buy our product because it's technically superior.
3. Customers will agree with our perception that the product is "great."
4. Customers run no risk in buying from us instead of continuing to buy from their past suppliers.
5. The product will sell itself.
6. Distributors are desperate to stock and service the product.
7. We can develop the product on time and on budget.
8. We will have no trouble attracting the right staff.
9. Competitors will respond rationally.
10. We can insulate our product from competition.
11. We will be able to hold down prices while gaining share rapidly.
12. The rest of our company will gladly support our strategy and provide help as needed.

---

*variable has changed.* Polaroid lost $200 million from Polavision instant movies by assuming that a three minute cassette costing $7 would compete effectively against a half-hour videotape costing $20. Polaroid implicitly assumed that the high cost of equipment for videotaping and playback would remain prohibitive for most consumers. Meanwhile, companies pursuing those technologies steadily drove down costs. (See the exhibit "Some dangerous implicit assumptions.")

### Discovery-Driven Planning: An Illustrative Case

Discovery-driven planning offers a systematic way to uncover the dangerous implicit assumptions that would otherwise slip unnoticed and thus unchallenged into the plan. The process imposes a strict discipline that is captured in four related documents: a *reverse income statement,* which models the basic economics of the business; *pro forma operations specs,* which lay out the operations needed to run the business; a *key assumptions checklist,* which is used to ensure that assumptions are checked; and a *milestone planning chart,* which specifies the assumptions to be tested at each project milestone. As the venture unfolds and new data are uncovered, each of the documents is updated.

To demonstrate how this tool works, we will apply it retrospectively to Kao Corporation's highly successful entry into the floppy disk business in 1988. We deliberately draw on no inside information about Kao or its planning process but instead use the kind of limited public knowledge that often is all that any company would have at the start of a new venture.

### The company

Japan's Kao Corporation was a successful supplier of surfactants to the magnetic-media (floppy disk) industry. In 1981, the company began to study the potential for becoming a player in floppy disks by leveraging the surfactant technology it had developed in its core businesses, soap and cosmetics. Kao's managers realized that they had learned enough process knowledge from their floppy disk customers to supplement their own skills in surface chemistry. They believed they could produce floppy disks at a much lower cost and higher quality than other companies offered at that time. Kao's surfactant competencies were particularly valuable because the quality of the floppy disk's surface is crucial for its reliability. For a company in a mature industry, the opportunity to move current product into a growth industry was highly attractive.

### The market

By the end of 1986, the demand for floppy disks was 500 million in the United States, 100 million in Europe, and 50 million in Japan, with growth estimated at 40% per year, compounded. This meant that by 1993, the global market would be approaching 3 billion disks, of which about a third would be in the original equipment manufacturer (OEM) market, namely such big-volume purchasers of disks as IBM, Apple, and Microsoft, which use disks to distribute their software. OEM industry prices were expected to be about 180 yen per disk by 1993. Quality and reliability have always been important product characteristics for OEMs such as software houses because defective disks have a devastating impact on customers' perceptions of the company's overall quality.

### The reverse income statement

Discovery-driven planning starts with the bottom line. For Kao, back when it began to consider its options, the question was whether the floppy disk venture had the potential to enhance the company's competitive position and financial performance significantly. If not, why should Kao incur the risk and uncertainty of a major strategic venture?

Here, we impose the first discipline, which is to plan the venture using a reverse income statement, which runs from the bottom line up. (See the exhibit, "First, start with a reverse income statement." The four exhibits referred to in the article are located in the sidebar, "How Kao Might Have Tackled Its New Venture.") Instead of starting with estimates of revenues and working down the income statement to derive profits, we start with *required profits*. We then work our way up the profit and loss to determine how much revenue it will take to deliver the level of profits we require and how much cost can be allowed. The underlying philosophy is to impose revenue and cost disciplines by baking profitability into the plan at the outset: Required profits equal necessary revenues minus allowable costs.

At Kao in 1988, management might have started with these figures: net sales, about 500 billion yen; income before taxes, about 40 billion yen; and return on sales (ROS), 7.5%. Given such figures, how big must the floppy disk opportunity be to justify Kao's attention? Every company will set its own hurdles. We believe that a strategic venture should have the potential to enhance total profits by at least 10%. Moreover, to compensate for the increased risk, it should deliver greater profitability than reinvesting in the existing businesses would. Again, for purposes of illustration, assume that Kao demands a risk premium of 33% greater profitability. Since Kao's return on sales is 7.5%, it will require 10%.

If we use the Kao data, we find that the required profit for the floppy disk venture would be 4 billion yen (10% × 40 billion). To deliver 4 billion yen in profit with a 10% return on sales implies a business with 40 billion yen in sales.

Assuming that, despite its superior quality, Kao will have to price competitively to gain share as a new entrant, it should set a target

# How Kao Might Have Tackled Its New Venture: Discovery-Driven Planning in Action

**THE GOAL HERE** is to determine the value of success quickly. If the venture can't deliver significant returns, it may not be worth the risk.

## First, start with a reverse income statement

### Total figures

Required profits to add 10% to total profits = 4 billion yen
Necessary revenues to deliver 10% sales margin = 40 billion yen
Allowable costs to deliver 10% sales margin = 36 billion yen

### Per unit figures

Required unit sales at 160 yen per unit = 250 million units
Necessary percentage of world market share of OEM unit sales = 25%
Allowable costs per unit for 10% sales margin = 144 yen

## Second, lay out all the activities needed to run the venture

### Pro forma operations specs

#### 1. Sales

Required disk sales = 250 million disks
Average order size (Assumption 8) = 10,000 disks
Orders required (250 million/10,000) = 25,000

Number of calls to make a sale (Assumption 9) = 4
Sales calls required (4 x 25,000) = 100,000 per year

Calls per day per salesperson (Assumption 10) = 2
Annual salesperson days (100,000/2) = 50,000
Sales force for 250 days per year (Assumption 11)
   50,000 salesperson days/250 = 200 people

Salary per salesperson = 10 million yen (Assumption 12)
   Total sales-force salary cost (10 million yen x 200) = 2 billion yen

#### 2. Manufacturing

Quality specification of disk surface: 50% fewer
   flaws than best competitor (Assumption 15)

Annual production capacity per line = 25 per minute
   x 1440 minutes per day x 348 days (Assumption 16)
   = 12.5 million disks

Production lines needed (250 million disks/12.5
  million disks per line) = 20 lines

Production staffing (30 per line [Assumption 17]
  x 20 lines) = 600 workers

Salary per worker = 5 million yen (Assumption 18)
Total production salaries (600 x 5 million yen) = 3 billion yen

Materials costs per disk = 20 yen (Assumption 19)
Total materials cost (20 x 250 million disks) = 5 billion yen

Packaging per 10 disks = 40 yen (Assumption 20)
Total packaging costs (40 x 25 million packages) =1 billion yen

3. Shipping

Containers needed per order of 10,000 disks = 1
  (Assumption 13)
Shipping cost per container = 100,000 yen
  (Assumption 14)
Total shipping costs (25,000 orders x 100,000 yen) = 2.5 billion yen

4. Equipment and depreciation

Fixed asset investment to sales = 1:1 (Assumption 5) = 40 billion yen
Equipment life = 3 years (Assumption 7)
Annual depreciation (40 billion yen/3 years) = 13.3 billion yen

Keeping a checklist is an important discipline to ensure that each assumption is flagged and tested as a venture unfolds.

## Third, track all assumptions

| Assumption | Measurement |
| --- | --- |
| 1. Profit margin | 10% of sales |
| 2. Revenues | 40 billion yen |
| 3. Unit selling price | 160 yen |
| 4. 1993 world OEM market | 1 billion disks |
| 5. Fixed asset investment to sales | 1:1 |
| 6. Effective production capacity per line | 25 disks per minute |
| 7. Effective life of equipment | 3 years |
| 8. Average OEM order size | 10,000 disks |
| 9. Sales calls per OEM order | 4 calls per order |
| 10. Sales calls per salesperson per day | 2 calls per day |
| 11. Selling days per year | 250 days |
| 12. Annual salesperson's salary | 10 million yen |
| 13. Containers required per order | 1 container |

(continued)

## How Kao Might Have Tackled Its New Venture: Discovery-Driven Planning in Action (continued)

| | |
|---|---|
| **14.** Shipping cost per container | 100,000 yen |
| **15.** Quality level needed to get customers to switch: % fewer flaws per disk than top competitor | 50% |
| **16.** Production days per year | 348 days |
| **17.** Workers per production line per day (10 per line for 3 shifts) | 30 per line |
| **18.** Annual manufacturing worker's salary | 5 million yen |
| **19.** Materials costs per disk | 20 yen |
| **20.** Packaging costs per 10 disks | 40 yen |
| **21.** Allowable administration costs (See revised reverse income statement, below) | 9.2 billion yen |

Now, with better data, one can see if the entire business proposition hangs together.

### Fourth, revise the reverse income statement

| | |
|---|---|
| **Required margin** | 10% return on sales |
| **Required profit** | 4 billion yen |
| **Necessary revenues** | 40 billion yen |
| **Allowable costs** | 36 billion yen |
| Sales-force salaries | 2.0 billion yen |
| Manufacturing salaries | 3.0 billion yen |
| Disk materials | 5.0 billion yen |
| Packaging | 1.0 billion yen |
| Shipping | 2.5 billion yen |
| Depreciation | 13.3 billion yen |
| Allowable administration and overhead costs | 9.2 billion yen (Assumption 21) |
| **Per-unit figures** | |
| Selling price | 160 yen |
| Total costs | 144 yen |
| Disk materials costs | 20 yen |

### Finally, plan to test assumptions at milestones

| Milestone event—namely, the completion of: | Assumptions to be tested |
|---|---|
| **1.** Initial data search and preliminary feasibility analysis | 4: 1993 world OEM market<br>8: Average OEM order size<br>9: Sales calls per OEM order |

10: Sales calls per salesperson per day
11: Salespeople needed for 250 selling days per year
12: Annual salesperson's salary
13: Containers required per order
14: Shipping cost per container
16: Production days per year
18: Annual manufacturing worker's salary

**2.** Prototype batches produced

15: Quality to get customers to switch
19: Materials costs per disk

**3.** Technical testing by customers

3: Unit selling price
15: Quality to get customers to switch

**4.** Subcontracted production

19: Materials costs per disk

**5.** Sales of subcontracted production

1: Profit margin
2: Revenues
3: Unit selling price
8: Average OEM order size
9: Sales calls per OEM order
10: Sales calls per salesperson per day
12: Annual salesperson's salary
15: Quality to get customers to switch

**6.** Purchase of an existing plant

5: Fixed asset investment to sales
7: Effective life of equipment

**7.** Pilot production at purchased plant

6: Effective production capacity per line
16: Production days per year
17: Workers per production line per day
18: Annual manufacturing worker's salary
19: Materials costs per disk
20: Packaging costs per 10 disks

**8.** Competitor reaction

1: Profit margin
2: Revenues
3: Unit selling price

**9.** Product redesign

19: Materials costs per disk
20: Packaging costs per 10 disks

**10.** Major repricing analysis

1: Profit margin
2: Revenues
3: Unit selling price
4: 1993 world OEM market

**11.** Plant redesign

5: Fixed asset investment to sales
6: Effective production capacity per line
19: Materials costs per disk

price of 160 yen per disk. That translates into unit sales of 250 million disks (40 billion yen in sales divided by 160 yen per disk). By imposing these simple performance measures at the start (1988), we quickly establish both the scale and scope of the venture: Kao would need to capture 25% of the total world OEM market (25% of 1 billion disks) by 1993. Given what is known about the size of the market, Kao clearly must be prepared to compete globally from the outset, making major commitments not only to manufacturing but also to selling.

Continuing up the profit and loss, we next calculate allowable costs: If Kao is to capture 10% margin on a price of 160 yen per disk, the total cost to manufacture, sell, and distribute the disks worldwide cannot exceed 144 yen per disk. The reverse income statement makes clear immediately that the challenge for the floppy disk venture will be to keep a lid on expenses.

### The pro forma operations specs and the assumptions checklist

The second discipline in the process is to construct pro forma operations specs laying out the activities required to produce, sell, service, and deliver the product or service to the customer. Together, those activities comprise the venture's allowable costs. At first, the operations specs can be modeled on a simple spreadsheet without investing in more than a few telephone calls or on-line searches to get basic data. If an idea holds together, it is possible to identify and test underlying assumptions, constantly fleshing out and correcting the model in light of new information. When a company uses this cumulative approach, major flaws in the business concept soon become obvious, and poor concepts can be abandoned long before significant investments are made.

We believe it is essential to use industry standards for building a realistic picture of what the business has to look like to be competitive. Every industry has its own pressures—which determine normal rates of return in that industry—as well as standard performance measures such as asset-to-sales ratios, industry profit margins, plant utilization, and so on. In a globally competitive environment, no sane manager should expect to escape the competitive discipline that is captured and measured in industry standards. These standards are readily available from investment analysts and business information services. In countries with information sources that are less well developed than those in the United States, key industry parameters are still used by investment bankers and, more specifically, by those commercial bankers who specialize in loans to the particular industry. For those getting into a new industry, the best approach is to adapt standards from similar industries.

Note that we do not begin with an elaborate analysis of product or service attributes or an in-depth market study. That comes later. Initially, we are simply trying to capture the venture's embedded assumptions. The basic discipline is to spell out clearly and realistically where the venture will have to match existing industry standards and in what one or two places managers expect to excel and how they expect to do so.

Kao's managers in 1988 might have considered performance standards for the floppy disk industry. Because there would be no reason to believe that Kao could use standard production equipment any better than established competitors could, it would want to plan to match industry performance on measures relating to equipment use. Kao would ascertain, for example, that the effective production capacity per line was 25 disks per minute in the industry; and the effective life of production equipment was three years. Kao's advantage was in surface chemistry and surface physics, which could improve quality and reduce the cost of materials, thus improving margins. When Kao planned its materials cost, it would want to turn that advantage into a specific challenge for manufacturing: Beat the industry standard for materials cost by 25%. The formal framing of operational challenges is an important step in discovery-driven planning. In our experience, people who are good in design and operations can be galvanized by clearly articulated challenges. That was the case at Canon, for example, when Keizo Yamaji challenged the engineers to develop a personal copier that required minimal service and cost less than $1,000, and the Canon engineers rose to the occasion.

A company can test the initial assumptions against experience with similar situations, the advice of experts in the industry, or published information sources. The point is not to demand the highest degree of accuracy but to build a reasonable model of the economics and logistics of the venture and to assess the order of magnitude of the challenges. Later, the company can analyze where the plan is most sensitive to wrong assumptions and do more formal checks. Consultants to the industry—bankers, suppliers, potential customers, and distributors— often can provide low-cost and surprisingly accurate information.

The company must build a picture of the activities that are needed to carry out the business and the costs. Hence in the pro forma operations specs, we ask how many orders are needed to deliver 250 million units in sales; then how many sales calls it will take to secure those orders; then how many salespeople it will take to make the sales calls, given the fact that they are selling to a global OEM market; then how much it will cost in sales-force compensation. (See the exhibit "Second, lay out all the activities needed to run the venture" located on the sidebar "How Kao Might Have Tackled Its New Venture.") Each assumption can be checked, at first somewhat roughly and then with increasing precision. Readers might disagree with our first-cut estimates. That is fine—so might Kao Corporation. Reasonable disagreement triggers discussion and, perhaps, adjustments to the spreadsheet. The evolving document is doing its job if it becomes the catalyst for such discussion.

The third discipline of discovery-driven planning is to compile an assumption checklist to ensure that each assumption is flagged, discussed, and checked as the venture unfolds. (See the exhibit "Third, track all assumptions.")

The entire process is looped back into a revised reverse income statement, in which one can see if the entire business proposition hangs together. (See the exhibit, "Fourth, revise the reverse income statement.") If it doesn't, the process must be repeated until the performance requirements and industry standards can be met; otherwise, the venture should be scrapped.

## Milestone planning

Conventional planning approaches tend to focus managers on meeting plan, usually an impossible goal for a venture rife with assumptions. It is also counterproductive—insistence on meeting plan actually prevents learning. Managers can formally plan to learn by using milestone events to test assumptions.

Milestone planning is by now a familiar technique for monitoring the progress of new ventures. The basic idea, as described by Zenas Block and Ian C. MacMillan in the book *Corporate Venturing* (Harvard Business School Press, 1993), is to postpone major commitments of resources until the evidence from the previous milestone event signals that the risk of taking the next step is justified. What we are proposing here is an expanded use of the tool to support the discipline of transforming assumptions into knowledge.

Going back to what Kao might have been thinking in 1988, recall that the floppy disk venture would require a 40-billion-yen investment in fixed assets alone. Before investing such a large sum, Kao would certainly have wanted to find ways to test the most critical assumptions underlying the three major challenges of the venture:

- capturing 25% global market share with a 20-yen-per-disk discount and superior quality;

- maintaining at least the same asset productivity as the average competitor and producing a floppy disk at 90% of the estimated total costs of existing competitors; and

- using superior raw materials and applied surface technology to produce superior-quality disks for 20 yen per unit instead of the industry standard of 27 yen per unit.

For serious challenges like those, it may be worth spending resources to create specific milestone events to test the assumptions before launching a 40-billion-yen venture. For instance, Kao might subcontract prototype production so that sophisticated OEM customers could conduct technical tests on the proposed disk. If the prototypes survive the tests, then, rather than rest on the assumption that it can capture significant business at the target price, Kao might subcontract production of a large batch of floppy disks for resale to customers. It could thus test the appetite of the OEM market for price discounting from a newcomer.

Similarly, for testing its ability to cope with the second and third challenges once the Kao prototype has been developed, it might be worthwhile to buy out a small existing floppy disk manufacturer and apply the technology in an established plant rather than try to start up a greenfield operation. Once Kao can demonstrate its ability to produce disks at the required quality and cost in the small plant, it can move ahead with its own full-scale plants.

Deliberate assumption-testing milestones are depicted in the exhibit "Finally, Plan to Test Assumptions at Milestones," which also shows some of the other typical milestones that occur in most major ventures. The assumptions that should be tested at each milestone are listed with appropriate numbers from the assumption checklist.

In practice, it is wise to designate a *keeper of the assumptions*—someone whose formal task is to ensure that assumptions are checked and updated as each milestone is reached and that the revised assumptions are incorporated into successive iterations of the four discovery-driven planning documents. Without a specific person dedicated to following up, it is highly unlikely that individuals, up to their armpits in project pressures, will be able to coordinate the updating independently.

Discovery-driven planning is a powerful tool for any significant strategic undertaking that is fraught with uncertainty—new-product or market ventures, technology development, joint ventures, strategic alliances, even major systems redevelopment. Unlike platform-based planning, in which much is known, discovery-driven planning forces managers to articulate what they don't know, and it forces a discipline for learning. As a planning tool, it thus raises the visibility of the make-or-break uncertainties common to new ventures and helps managers address them at the lowest possible cost.

**Note**

The authors wish to thank Shiuchi Matsuda of Waseda University's Entrepreneurial Research Unit for providing case material on Kao's floppy disk venture.

**Originally published in July 1995. Reprint** 95406

# The Discipline
# of Innovation

*by Peter F. Drucker*

DESPITE MUCH DISCUSSION THESE days of the "entrepreneurial person-ality," few of the entrepreneurs with whom I have worked during the past 30 years had such personalities. But I have known many people—salespeople, surgeons, journalists, scholars, even musicians—who did have them without being the least bit entrepreneurial. What all the successful entrepreneurs I have met have in common is not a certain kind of personality but a commitment to the systematic practice of innovation.

Innovation is the specific function of entrepreneurship, whether in an existing business, a public service institution, or a new venture started by a lone individual in the family kitchen. It is the means by which the entrepreneur either creates new wealth-producing resour-ces or endows existing resources with enhanced potential for creating wealth.

Today, much confusion exists about the proper definition of entrepreneurship. Some observers use the term to refer to all small businesses; others, to all new businesses. In practice, however, a great many well-established businesses engage in highly successful entrepreneurship. The term, then, refers not to an enterprise's size or age but to a certain kind of activity. At the heart of that activity is innovation: the effort to create purposeful, focused change in an enterprise's economic or social potential.

## Sources of Innovation

There are, of course, innovations that spring from a flash of genius. Most innovations, however, especially the successful ones, result from a conscious, purposeful search for innovation opportunities, which are found only in a few situations. Four such areas of opportunity exist within a company or industry: unexpected occurrences, incongruities, process needs, and industry and market changes.

Three additional sources of opportunity exist outside a company in its social and intellectual environment: demographic changes, changes in perception, and new knowledge.

True, these sources overlap, different as they may be in the nature of their risk, difficulty, and complexity, and the potential for innovation may well lie in more than one area at a time. But together, they account for the great majority of all innovation opportunities.

### 1. Unexpected occurrences

Consider, first, the easiest and simplest source of innovation opportunity: the unexpected. In the early 1930s, IBM developed the first modern accounting machine, which was designed for banks. But banks in 1933 did not buy new equipment. What saved the company— according to a story that Thomas Watson, Sr., the company's founder and long-term CEO, often told—was its exploitation of an unexpected success: The New York Public Library wanted to buy a machine. Unlike the banks, libraries in those early New Deal days had money, and Watson sold more than a hundred of his otherwise unsalable machines to libraries.

Fifteen years later, when everyone believed that computers were designed for advanced scientific work, business unexpectedly showed an interest in a machine that could do payroll. Univac, which had the most advanced machine, spurned business applications. But IBM immediately realized it faced a possible unexpected success, redesigned what was basically Univac's machine for such mundane applications as payroll, and within five years became a leader in the computer industry, a position it has maintained to this day.

## Idea in Brief

In the hypercompetition for breakthrough solutions, managers worry too much about characteristics and personality—"Am I smart enough? Do I have the right temperament?"—and not enough about process. A commitment to the systematic search for imaginative and useful ideas is what successful entrepreneurs share—not some special genius or trait. What's more, entrepreneurship can occur in a business of any size or age because, at heart, it has to do with a certain kind of activity: innovation, the disciplined effort to improve a business's potential.

Most innovations result from a conscious, purposeful search for opportunities—within the company and the industry as well as the larger social and intellectual environment. A successful innovation may come from pulling together different strands of knowledge, recognizing an underlying theme in public perception, or extracting new insights from failure.

The key is to know where to look.

The unexpected failure may be an equally important source of innovation opportunities. Everyone knows about the Ford Edsel as the biggest new-car failure in automotive history. What very few people seem to know, however, is that the Edsel's failure was the foundation for much of the company's later success. Ford planned the Edsel, the most carefully designed car to that point in American automotive history, to give the company a full product line with which to compete with General Motors. When it bombed, despite all the planning, market research, and design that had gone into it, Ford realized that something was happening in the automobile market that ran counter to the basic assumptions on which GM and everyone else had been designing and marketing cars. No longer was the market segmented primarily by income groups; the new principle of segmentation was what we now call "lifestyles." Ford's response was the Mustang, a car that gave the company a distinct personality and reestablished it as an industry leader.

Unexpected successes and failures are such productive sources of innovation opportunities because most businesses dismiss them,

# Idea in Practice

Successful entrepreneurs don't wait for innovative ideas to strike like a lightning bolt. They go out looking for innovation opportunities in seven key areas:

1. **Unexpected occurrences.** These often include failures. Few people know, for instance, that the failure of the Edsel led Ford to realize that the auto market was now segmented by lifestyle instead of by income group. Ford's response was the Mustang, and an auto legend was born.

2. **Incongruities.** By the 1960s, cataract removal had become high-tech, except for cutting a ligament, an "old-fashioned" step that was uncomfortable for eye surgeons. Alcon Laboratories responded by modifying an enzyme that dissolved the ligament. Surgeons immediately accepted the new product, giving Alcon a monopoly.

3. **Process needs.** Two process innovations developed around 1890 created "the media" as we know it today: linotype made it possible to produce newspapers quickly, and advertising made it possible to distribute news practically free of charge.

4. **Industry and market changes.** The brokerage firm Donaldson, Lufkin & Jenrette achieved fabulous success because its founders recognized that the emerging market for institutional investors would one day predominate in the industry.

disregard them, and even resent them. The German scientist who around 1905 synthesized novocaine, the first nonaddictive narcotic, had intended it to be used in major surgical procedures like amputation. Surgeons, however, preferred total anesthesia for such procedures; they still do. Instead, novocaine found a ready appeal among dentists. Its inventor spent the remaining years of his life traveling from dental school to dental school making speeches that forbade dentists from "misusing" his noble invention in applications for which he had not intended it.

This is a caricature, to be sure, but it illustrates the attitude managers often take to the unexpected: "It should not have happened." Corporate reporting systems further ingrain this reaction, for they draw attention away from unanticipated possibilities. The typical

5. **Demographic changes.** Why are the Japanese ahead in robotics? Around 1970, everyone knew that there was both a baby bust and an education explosion, such that the number of blue-collar manufacturing workers would decline. Everyone knew—but only the Japanese took action.

6. **Changes in perception.** Such changes don't alter the facts, but can dramatically change their meaning. Americans' health has never been better—yet we're obsessed with preventing disease and staying fit. Innovators who understand our *perception* of health have launched magazines, introduced health foods, and started exercise classes.

7. **New knowledge.** Knowledge-based innovations require long lead times and the convergence of different kinds of knowledge. The computer required knowledge that was available by 1918, but the first operational digital computer did not appear until 1946.

Purposeful innovation begins with looking, asking, and listening. Talent and expert knowledge help, but don't be deluded by all the stories about flashes of insight. The key task is to work out analytically what the innovation has to be in order to satisfy a particular opportunity.

monthly or quarterly report has on its first page a list of problems—that is, the areas where results fall short of expectations. Such information is needed, of course, to help prevent deterioration of performance. But it also suppresses the recognition of new opportunities. The first acknowledgment of a possible opportunity usually applies to an area in which a company does better than budgeted. Thus genuinely entrepreneurial businesses have two "first pages"—a problem page and an opportunity page—and managers spend equal time on both.

## 2. Incongruities

Alcon Laboratories was one of the success stories of the 1960s because Bill Conner, the company's cofounder, exploited an incongruity in medical technology. The cataract operation is the world's third or fourth most common surgical procedure. During the past 300 years, doctors systematized it to the point that the only "old-fashioned" step left was the cutting of a ligament. Eye surgeons had learned to cut the ligament with complete success, but it was so different a procedure from the rest of the operation, and so incompatible with it, that they often dreaded it. It was incongruous.

Doctors had known for 50 years about an enzyme that could dissolve the ligament without cutting. All Conner did was to add a preservative to this enzyme that gave it a few months' shelf life. Eye surgeons immediately accepted the new compound, and Alcon found itself with a worldwide monopoly. Fifteen years later, Nestlé bought the company for a fancy price.

Such an incongruity within the logic or rhythm of a process is only one possibility out of which innovation opportunities may arise. Another source is incongruity between economic realities. For instance, whenever an industry has a steadily growing market but falling profit margins—as, say, in the steel industries of developed countries between 1950 and 1970—an incongruity exists. The innovative response: minimills.

An incongruity between expectations and results can also open up possibilities for innovation. For 50 years after the turn of the century, shipbuilders and shipping companies worked hard both to make ships faster and to lower their fuel consumption. Even so, the more successful they were in boosting speed and trimming their fuel needs, the worse the economics of ocean freighters became. By 1950 or so, the ocean freighter was dying, if not already dead.

All that was wrong, however, was an incongruity between the industry's assumptions and its realities. The real costs did not come from doing work (that is, being at sea) but from *not* doing work (that is, sitting idle in port). Once managers understood where costs truly lay, the innovations were obvious: the roll-on and roll-off ship and the container ship. These solutions, which involved old technology, simply applied to the ocean freighter what railroads and truckers had been using for 30 years. A shift in viewpoint, not in technology, totally changed the economics of ocean shipping and turned it into one of the major growth industries of the last 20 to 30 years.

### 3. Process needs

Anyone who has ever driven in Japan knows that the country has no modern highway system. Its roads still follow the paths laid down for—or by—oxcarts in the tenth century. What makes the system work for automobiles and trucks is an adaptation of the reflector used on American highways since the early 1930s. The reflector lets each car see which other cars are approaching from any one of a half-dozen directions. This minor invention, which enables traffic to move smoothly and with a minimum of accidents, exploited a process need.

What we now call the media had its origin in two innovations developed around 1890 in response to process needs. One was Ottmar Mergenthaler's Linotype, which made it possible to produce newspapers quickly and in large volume. The other was a social innovation, modern advertising, invented by the first true newspaper publishers, Adolph Ochs of the *New York Times,* Joseph Pulitzer of the *New York World,* and William Randolph Hearst. Advertising made it possible for them to distribute news practically free of charge, with the profit coming from marketing.

### 4. Industry and market changes

Managers may believe that industry structures are ordained by the good Lord, but these structures can—and often do—change overnight. Such change creates tremendous opportunity for innovation.

One of American business's great success stories in recent decades is the brokerage firm of Donaldson, Lufkin & Jenrette, recently acquired by the Equitable Life Assurance Society. DL&J was founded in 1960 by three young men, all graduates of the Harvard Business School, who realized that the structure of the financial industry was changing as institutional investors became dominant. These young men had practically no capital and no connections. Still, within a few years, their firm had become a leader in the move to negotiated commissions and one of Wall Street's stellar performers. It was the first to be incorporated and go public.

In a similar fashion, changes in industry structure have created massive innovation opportunities for American health care providers. During the past ten or 15 years, independent surgical and psychiatric clinics, emergency centers, and HMOs have opened throughout the country. Comparable opportunities in telecommunications followed industry upheavals—in transmission (with the emergence of MCI and Sprint in long-distance service) and in equipment (with the emergence of such companies as Rolm in the manufacturing of private branch exchanges).

When an industry grows quickly—the critical figure seems to be in the neighborhood of 40% growth in ten years or less—its structure changes. Established companies, concentrating on defending what they already have, tend not to counterattack when a newcomer challenges them. Indeed, when market or industry structures change, traditional industry leaders again and again neglect the fastest growing market segments. New opportunities rarely fit the way the industry has always approached the market, defined it, or organized to serve it. Innovators therefore have a good chance of being left alone for a long time.

### 5. Demographic changes

Of the outside sources of innovation opportunities, demographics are the most reliable. Demographic events have known lead times; for instance, every person who will be in the American labor force by the year 2000 has already been born. Yet because policy makers often neglect demographics, those who watch them and exploit them can reap great rewards.

The Japanese are ahead in robotics because they paid attention to demographics. Everyone in the developed countries around 1970 or so knew that there was both a baby bust and an education explosion going on; about half or more of the young people were staying in school beyond high school. Consequently, the number of people available for traditional blue-collar work in manufacturing was bound to decrease and become inadequate by 1990. Everyone knew this, but only the Japanese acted on it, and they now have a ten-year lead in robotics.

Much the same is true of Club Mediterranee's success in the travel and resort business. By 1970, thoughtful observers could have seen the emergence of large numbers of affluent and educated young adults in Europe and the United States. Not comfortable with the kind of vacations their working-class parents had enjoyed—the summer weeks at Brighton or Atlantic City—these young people were ideal customers for a new and exotic version of the "hangout" of their teen years.

Managers have known for a long time that demographics matter, but they have always believed that population statistics change slowly. In this century, however, they don't. Indeed, the innovation opportunities made possible by changes in the numbers of people— and in their age distribution, education, occupations, and geographic location—are among the most rewarding and least risky of entrepreneurial pursuits.

## 6. Changes in perception

"The glass is half full" and "The glass is half empty" are descriptions of the same phenomenon but have vastly different meanings. Changing a manager's perception of a glass from half full to half empty opens up big innovation opportunities.

All factual evidence indicates, for instance, that in the last 20 years, Americans' health has improved with unprecedented speed— whether measured by mortality rates for the newborn, survival rates for the very old, the incidence of cancers (other than lung cancer), cancer cure rates, or other factors. Even so, collective hypochondria grips the nation. Never before has there been so much concern with or fear about health. Suddenly, everything seems to cause cancer or degenerative heart disease or premature loss of memory. The glass is clearly half empty.

Rather than rejoicing in great improvements in health, Americans seem to be emphasizing how far away they still are from immortality. This view of things has created many opportunities for innovations: markets for new health care magazines, for exercise classes and jogging equipment, and for all kinds of health foods. The fastest growing new U.S. business in 1983 was a company that makes indoor exercise equipment.

A change in perception does not alter facts. It changes their meaning, though—and very quickly. It took less than two years for the computer to change from being perceived as a threat and as something only big businesses would use to something one buys for doing income tax. Economics do not necessarily dictate such a change; in fact, they may be irrelevant. What determines whether people see a glass as half full or half empty is mood rather than fact, and a change in mood often defies quantification. But it is not exotic. It is concrete. It can be defined. It can be tested. And it can be exploited for innovation opportunity.

### 7. New knowledge

Among history-making innovations, those that are based on new knowledge—whether scientific, technical, or social—rank high. They are the superstars of entrepreneurship; they get the publicity and the money. They are what people usually mean when they talk of innovation, although not all innovations based on knowledge are important.

Knowledge-based innovations differ from all others in the time they take, in their casualty rates, and in their predictability, as well as in the challenges they pose to entrepreneurs. Like most superstars, they can be temperamental, capricious, and hard to direct. They have, for instance, the longest lead time of all innovations. There is a protracted span between the emergence of new knowledge and its distillation into usable technology. Then there is another long period before this new technology appears in the marketplace in products, processes, or services. Overall, the lead time involved is something like 50 years, a figure that has not shortened appreciably throughout history.

To become effective, innovation of this sort usually demands not one kind of knowledge but many. Consider one of the most potent knowledge-based innovations: modern banking. The theory of the entrepreneurial bank—that is, of the purposeful use of capital to generate economic development—was formulated by the Comte de Saint-Simon during the era of Napoleon. Despite Saint-Simon's extraordinary prominence, it was not until 30 years after his death in

1825 that two of his disciples, the brothers Jacob and Isaac Pereire, established the first entrepreneurial bank, the Credit Mobilier, and ushered in what we now call finance capitalism.

The Pereires, however, did not know modern commercial banking, which developed at about the same time across the channel in England. The Credit Mobilier failed ignominiously. A few years later, two young men—one an American, J.P. Morgan, and one a German, Georg Siemens—put together the French theory of entrepreneurial banking and the English theory of commercial banking to create the first successful modern banks: J.P. Morgan & Company in New York, and the Deutsche Bank in Berlin. Ten years later, a young Japanese, Shibusawa Eiichi, adapted Siemens's concept to his country and thereby laid the foundation of Japan's modern economy. This is how knowledge-based innovation always works.

The computer, to cite another example, required no fewer than six separate strands of knowledge:

- binary arithmetic;

- Charles Babbage's conception of a calculating machine, in the first half of the nineteenth century;

- the punch card, invented by Herman Hollerith for the U.S. census of 1890;

- the audion tube, an electronic switch invented in 1906;

- symbolic logic, which was developed between 1910 and 1913 by Bertrand Russell and Alfred North Whitehead;

- and concepts of programming and feedback that came out of abortive attempts during World War I to develop effective anti-aircraft guns.

Although all the necessary knowledge was available by 1918, the first operational digital computer did not appear until 1946.

Long lead times and the need for convergence among different kinds of knowledge explain the peculiar rhythm of knowledge-based innovation, its attractions, and its dangers. During a long gestation period, there is a lot of talk and little action. Then, when all the elements suddenly converge, there is tremendous excitement and activity and an enormous amount of speculation. Between 1880 and 1890, for example, almost 1,000 electric-apparatus companies were founded in developed countries. Then, as always, there was a crash and a shakeout. By 1914, only 25 were still alive. In the early 1920s, 300 to 500 automobile companies existed in the United States; by 1960, only four of them remained.

It may be difficult, but knowledge-based innovation can be managed. Success requires careful analysis of the various kinds of knowledge needed to make an innovation possible. Both J.P. Morgan and Georg Siemens did this when they established their banking ventures. The Wright brothers did this when they developed the first operational airplane.

Careful analysis of the needs—and, above all, the capabilities—of the intended user is also essential. It may seem paradoxical, but knowledge-based innovation is more market dependent than any other kind of innovation. De Havilland, a British company, designed and built the first passenger jet, but it did not analyze what the market needed and therefore did not identify two key factors. One was configuration—that is, the right size with the right payload for the routes on which a jet would give an airline the greatest advantage. The other was equally mundane: How could the airlines finance the purchase of such an expensive plane? Because de Havilland failed to do an adequate user analysis, two American companies, Boeing and Douglas, took over the commercial jet-aircraft industry.

## Principles of Innovation

Purposeful, systematic innovation begins with the analysis of the sources of new opportunities. Depending on the context, sources will have different importance at different times. Demographics, for instance, may be of little concern to innovators of fundamental industrial processes like steelmaking, although the Linotype machine became successful primarily because there were not enough skilled typesetters available to satisfy a mass market. By the same token, new knowledge may be of little relevance to someone innovating a social instrument to satisfy a need that changing demographics or tax laws have created. But whatever the situation, innovators must analyze all opportunity sources.

Because innovation is both conceptual and perceptual, would-be innovators must also go out and look, ask, and listen. Successful innovators use both the right and left sides of their brains. They work out analytically what the innovation has to be to satisfy an opportunity. Then they go out and look at potential users to study their expectations, their values, and their needs.

To be effective, an innovation has to be simple, and it has to be focused. It should do only one thing; otherwise it confuses people. Indeed, the greatest praise an innovation can receive is for people to say, "This is obvious! Why didn't I think of it? It's so simple!" Even the innovation that creates new users and new markets should be directed toward a specific, clear, and carefully designed application.

Effective innovations start small. They are not grandiose. It may be to enable a moving vehicle to draw electric power while it runs along rails, the innovation that made possible the electric streetcar. Or it may be the elementary idea of putting the same number of matches into a matchbox (it used to be 50). This simple notion made possible the automatic filling of matchboxes and gave the Swedes a world monopoly on matches for half a century. By contrast, grandiose ideas for things that will "revolutionize an industry" are unlikely to work.

In fact, no one can foretell whether a given innovation will end up a big business or a modest achievement. But even if the results are modest, the successful innovation aims from the beginning to become the standard setter, to determine the direction of a new technology or a new industry, to create the business that is—and remains—ahead of the pack. If an innovation does not aim at leadership from the beginning, it is unlikely to be innovative enough.

Above all, innovation is work rather than genius. It requires knowledge. It often requires ingenuity. And it requires focus. There are clearly people who are more talented innovators than others, but their talents lie in well-defined areas. Indeed, innovators rarely work in more than one area. For all his systematic innovative accomplishments, Thomas Edison worked only in the electrical field. An innovator in financial areas, Citibank for example, is not likely to embark on innovations in health care.

In innovation, as in any other endeavor, there is talent, there is ingenuity, and there is knowledge. But when all is said and done, what innovation requires is hard, focused, purposeful work. If diligence, persistence, and commitment are lacking, talent, ingenuity, and knowledge are of no avail.

There is, of course, far more to entrepreneurship than systematic innovation—distinct entrepreneurial strategies, for example, and the principles of entrepreneurial management, which are needed equally in the established enterprise, the public service organization, and the new venture. But the very foundation of entrepreneurship is the practice of systematic innovation.

**Originally published in May 1985.  Reprint** 3480

# Innovation Killers

How Financial Tools Destroy Your Capacity to Do New Things. *by Clayton M. Christensen, Stephen P. Kaufman, and Willy C. Shih*

**FOR YEARS WE'VE BEEN** puzzling about why so many smart, hardworking managers in well-run companies find it impossible to innovate successfully. Our investigations have uncovered a number of culprits, which we've discussed in earlier books and articles. These include paying too much attention to the company's most profitable customers (thereby leaving less-demanding customers at risk) and creating new products that don't help customers do the jobs they want to do. Now we'd like to name the misguided application of three financial-analysis tools as an accomplice in the conspiracy against successful innovation. We allege crimes against these suspects:

- The use of discounted cash flow (DCF) and net present value (NPV) to evaluate investment opportunities causes managers to underestimate the real returns and benefits of proceeding with investments in innovation.

- The way that fixed and sunk costs are considered when evaluating future investments confers an unfair advantage on challengers and shackles incumbent firms that attempt to respond to an attack.

- The emphasis on earnings per share as the primary driver of share price and hence of shareholder value creation, to the exclusion of almost everything else, diverts resources away from investments whose payoff lies beyond the immediate horizon.

These are not bad tools and concepts, we hasten to add. But the way they are commonly wielded in evaluating investments creates a systematic bias against innovation. We will recommend alternative methods that, in our experience, can help managers innovate with a much more astute eye for future value. Our primary aim, though, is simply to bring these concerns to light in the hope that others with deeper expertise may be inspired to examine and resolve them.

## Misapplying Discounted Cash Flow and Net Present Value

The first of the misleading and misapplied tools of financial analysis is the method of discounting cash flow to calculate the net present value of an initiative. Discounting a future stream of cash flows into a "present value" assumes that a rational investor would be indifferent to having a dollar today or to receiving some years from now a dollar plus the interest or return that could be earned by investing that dollar for those years. With that as an operating principle, it makes perfect sense to assess investments by dividing the money to be received in future years by $(1 + r)^n$, where $r$ is the discount rate—the annual return from investing that money—and $n$ is the number of years during which the investment could be earning that return.

While the mathematics of discounting is logically impeccable, analysts commonly commit two errors that create an anti-innovation bias. The first error is to assume that the base case of not investing in the innovation—the do-nothing scenario against which cash flows from the innovation are compared—is that the present health of the company will persist indefinitely into the future if the investment is not made. As shown in the exhibit "The DCF trap," the mathematics considers the investment in isolation and compares the present value of the innovation's cash stream less project costs with the cash stream in the absence of the investment, which is assumed to be unchanging.

# Idea in Brief

Most companies aren't half as innovative as their senior executives want them to be (or as their marketing claims suggest they are). What's stifling innovation? There are plenty of usual suspects, but the authors finger three financial tools as key accomplices. Discounted cash flow and net present value, as commonly used, underestimate the real returns and benefits of proceeding with an investment. Most executives compare the cash flows from innovation against the default scenario of doing nothing, assuming—incorrectly—that the present health of the company will persist indefinitely if the investment is not made. In most situations, however, competitors' sustaining and disruptive investments over time result in deterioration of financial performance. Fixed- and sunk-cost conventional wisdom confers an unfair advantage on challengers and shackles incumbent firms that attempt to respond to an attack. Executives in established companies, bemoaning the expense of building new brands and developing new sales and distribution channels, seek instead to leverage their existing brands and structures. Entrants, in contrast, simply create new ones. The problem for the incumbent isn't that the challenger can spend more; it's that the challenger is spared the dilemma of having to choose between full-cost and marginal-cost options. The emphasis on short-term earnings per share as the primary driver of share price, and hence shareholder value creation, acts to restrict investments in innovative long-term growth opportunities. These are not bad tools and concepts in and of themselves, but the way they are used to evaluate investments creates a systematic bias against successful innovation. The authors recommend alternative methods that can help managers innovate with a much more astute eye for future value.

In most situations, however, competitors' sustaining and disruptive investments over time result in price and margin pressure, technology changes, market share losses, sales volume decreases, and a declining stock price. As Eileen Rudden at Boston Consulting Group pointed out, the most likely stream of cash for the company in the do-nothing scenario is not a continuation of the status quo. It is a nonlinear decline in performance.

It's tempting but wrong to assess the value of a proposed investment by measuring whether it will make us better off than we are

---

## The DCF trap

*Most executives compare the cash flows from innovation against the default scenario of doing nothing, assuming—incorrectly—that the present health of the company will persist indefinitely if the investment is not made. For a better assessment of the innovation's value, the comparison should be between its projected discounted cash flow and the more likely scenario of a decline in performance in the absence of innovation investment.*

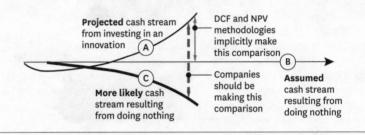

---

now. It's wrong because, if things are deteriorating on their own, we might be worse off than we are now after we make the proposed investment but better off than we would have been without it. Philip Bobbitt calls this logic Parmenides' Fallacy, after the ancient Greek logician who claimed to have proved that conditions in the real world must necessarily be unchanging. Analysts who attempt to distill the value of an innovation into one simple number that they can compare with other simple numbers are generally trapped by Parmenides' Fallacy.

It's hard to accurately forecast the stream of cash from an investment in innovation. It is even more difficult to forecast the extent to which a firm's financial performance may deteriorate in the absence of the investment. But this analysis must be done. Remember the response that good economists are taught to offer to the question "How are you?" It is "Relative to what?" This is a crucial question. Answering it entails assessing the projected value of the innovation against a range of scenarios, the most realistic of which is often a deteriorating competitive and financial future.

The second set of problems with discounted cash flow calculations relates to errors of estimation. Future cash flows, especially those generated by disruptive investments, are difficult to predict. Numbers for the "out years" can be a complete shot in the dark. To cope with what cannot be known, analysts often project a year-by-year stream of numbers for three to five years and then "punt" by calculating a terminal value to account for everything thereafter. The logic, of course, is that the year-to-year estimates for distant years are so imprecise as to be no more accurate than a terminal value. To calculate a terminal value, analysts divide the cash to be generated in the last year for which they've done a specific estimate by ($r$–$g$), the discount rate minus the projected growth rate in cash flows from that time on. They then discount that single number back to the present. In our experience, assumed terminal values often account for more than half of a project's total NPV.

Terminal value numbers, based as they are on estimates for preceding years, tend to amplify errors contained in early-year assumptions. More worrisome still, terminal value doesn't allow for the scenario testing that we described above—contrasting the result of this investment with the deterioration in performance that is the most likely result of doing nothing. And yet, because of market inertia, competitors' development cycles, and the typical pace of disruption, it is often in the fifth year or beyond—the point at which terminal value factors in—that the decline of the enterprise in the do-nothing scenario begins to accelerate.

Arguably, a root cause of companies' persistent underinvestment in the innovations required to sustain long-term success is the indiscriminate and oversimplified use of NPV as an analytical tool. Still, we understand the desire to quantify streams of cash that defy quantification and then to distill those streams into a single number that can be compared with other single numbers: It is an attempt to translate cacophonous articulations of the future into a language—numbers—that everyone can read and compare. We hope to show that numbers are not the only language into which the value of future investments can be translated—and that there are, in fact, other, better languages that all members of a management team can understand.

## Using Fixed and Sunk Costs Unwisely

The second widely misapplied paradigm of financial decision making relates to fixed and sunk costs. When evaluating a future course of action, the argument goes, managers should consider only the future or marginal cash outlays (either capital or expense) that are required for an innovation investment, subtract those outlays from the marginal cash that is likely to flow in, and discount the resulting net flow to the present. As with the paradigm of DCF and NPV, there is nothing wrong with the mathematics of this principle— as long as the capabilities required for yesterday's success are adequate for tomorrow's as well. When new capabilities are required for future success, however, this margining on fixed and sunk costs biases managers toward leveraging assets and capabilities that are likely to become obsolete.

For the purposes of this discussion we'll define fixed costs as those whose level is independent of the level of output. Typical fixed costs include general and administrative costs: salaries and benefits, insurance, taxes, and so on. (Variable costs include things like raw materials, commissions, and pay to temporary workers.) Sunk costs are those portions of fixed costs that are irrevocably committed, typically including investments in buildings and capital equipment and R&D costs.

An example from the steel industry illustrates how fixed and sunk costs make it difficult for companies that can and should invest in new capabilities actually to do so. In the late 1960s, steel minimills such as Nucor and Chaparral began disrupting integrated steelmakers such as U.S. Steel (USX), picking off customers in the least-demanding product tiers of each market and then moving relentlessly upmarket, using their 20% cost advantage to capture first the rebar market and then the bar and rod, angle iron, and structural beam markets. By 1988 the minimills had driven the higher-cost integrated mills out of lower-tier products, and Nucor had begun building its first minimill to roll sheet steel in Crawfordsville, Indiana. Nucor estimated that for an investment of $260 million it could sell 800,000 tons of steel annually at a price of $350 per ton. The cash cost to produce a ton of sheet steel in the Crawfordsville mill would be $270. When the timing of cash flows was taken into account, the internal rate of return to Nucor on this investment was over 20%—substantially higher than Nucor's weighted average cost of capital.

Incumbent USX recognized that the minimills constituted a grave threat. Using a new technology called continuous strip production, Nucor had now entered the sheet steel market, albeit with an inferior-quality product, at a significantly lower cost per ton. And Nucor's track record of vigilant improvement meant that the quality of its sheet steel would improve with production experience. Despite this understanding, USX engineers did not even consider building a greenfield minimill like the one Nucor built. The reason? It seemed more profitable to leverage the old technology than to create the new. USX's existing mills, which used traditional technology, had 30% excess capacity, and the marginal cash cost of producing an extra ton of steel by leveraging that excess capacity was less than $50 per ton. When USX's financial analysts contrasted the marginal cash flow of $300 ($350 revenue minus the $50 marginal cost) with the average cash flow of $80 per ton in a greenfield mill, investment in a new low-cost minimill made no sense. What's more, USX's plants were depreciated, so the marginal cash flow of $300 on a low asset base looked very attractive.

And therein lies the rub. Nucor, the attacker, had no fixed or sunk cost investments on which to do a marginal cost calculation. To Nucor, the full cost was the marginal cost. Crawfordsville was the only choice on its menu—and because the IRR was attractive, the decision was simple. USX, in contrast, had two choices on its menu: It could build a greenfield plant like Nucor's with a lower average cost per ton or it could utilize more fully its existing facility.

So what happened? Nucor has continued to improve its process, move upmarket, and gain market share with more efficient continuous strip production capabilities, while USX has relied on the capabilities that had been built to succeed in the past. USX's strategy to maximize marginal profit, in other words, caused the company not to minimize long-term average costs. As a result, the company is locked into an escalating cycle of commitment to a failing strategy.

The attractiveness of any investment can be completely assessed only when it is compared with the attractiveness of the right alternatives on a menu of investments. When a company is looking at adding capacity that is identical to existing capacity, it makes sense to compare the marginal cost of leveraging the old with the full cost of creating the new. But when new technologies or capabilities are required for future competitiveness, margining on the past will send you down the wrong path. The argument that investment decisions should be based on marginal costs is always correct. But when creating new capabilities is the issue, the relevant marginal cost is actually the full cost of creating the new.

When we look at fixed and sunk costs from this perspective, several anomalies we have observed in our studies of innovation are explained. Executives in established companies bemoan how expensive it is to build new brands and develop new sales and distribution channels—so they seek instead to leverage their existing brands and structures. Entrants, in contrast, simply create new ones. The problem for the incumbent isn't that the challenger can outspend it; it's that the challenger is spared the dilemma of having to choose between full-cost and marginal-cost options. We have repeatedly observed leading, established companies misapply fixed-and-sunk-cost doctrine and rely on assets and capabilities that were forged in the past to succeed in the future. In doing so, they fail to make the same investments that entrants and attackers find to be profitable.

A related misused financial practice that biases managers against investment in needed future capabilities is that of using a capital asset's estimated *usable* lifetime as the period over which it should be depreciated. This causes problems when the asset's usable lifetime is longer than its *competitive* lifetime. Managers who depreciate assets according to the more gradual schedule of usable life often face massive write-offs when those assets become competitively obsolete and need to be replaced with newer-technology assets. This was the situation confronting the integrated steelmakers. When building new capabilities entails writing off the old, incumbents face a hit to quarterly earnings that disruptive entrants to the industry do not. Knowing that the equity markets will punish them for a write-off, managers may stall in adopting new technology.

This may be part of the reason for the dramatic increase in private equity buyouts over the past decade and the recent surge of interest in technology-oriented industries. As disruptions continue to shorten the competitive lifetime of major investments made only three to five years ago, more companies find themselves needing to take asset write-downs or to significantly restructure their business models. These are wrenching changes that are often made more easily and comfortably outside the glare of the public markets.

What's the solution to this dilemma? Michael Mauboussin at Legg Mason Capital Management suggests it is to value *strategies,* not projects. When an attacker is gaining ground, executives at the incumbent companies need to do their investment analyses in the same way the attackers do—by focusing on the strategies that will ensure long-term competitiveness. This is the only way they can see the world as the attackers see it and the only way they can predict the consequences of not investing.

No manager would consciously decide to destroy a company by leveraging the competencies of the past while ignoring those required for the future. Yet this is precisely what many of them do. They do it because strategy and finance were taught as separate topics in business school. Their professors of financial modeling alluded to the importance of strategy, and their strategy professors occasionally referred to value creation, but little time was spent on a thoughtful integration of the two. This bifurcation persists in most companies, where responsibilities for strategy and finance reside in the realms of different vice presidents. Because a firm's actual strategy is defined by the stream of projects in which it does or doesn't invest, finance and strategy need to be studied and practiced in an integrated way.

## Focusing Myopically on Earnings per Share

A third financial paradigm that leads established companies to underinvest in innovation is the emphasis on earnings per share as the primary driver of share price and hence of shareholder value creation. Managers are under so much pressure, from various directions, to focus on short-term stock performance that they pay less attention to the company's long-term health than they might—to the point where they're reluctant to invest in innovations that don't pay off immediately.

Where's the pressure coming from? To answer that question, we need to look briefly at the principal-agent theory—the doctrine that the interests of shareholders (principals) aren't aligned with those of managers (agents). Without powerful financial incentives to focus the interests of principals and agents on maximizing shareholder value, the thinking goes, agents will pursue other agendas—and in the process, may neglect to pay enough attention to efficiencies or squander capital investments on pet projects—at the expense of profits that ought to accrue to the principals.

That conflict of incentives has been taught so aggressively that the compensation of most senior executives in publicly traded companies is now heavily weighted away from salaries and toward packages that reward improvements in share price. That in turn has led to an almost singular focus on earnings per share and EPS growth as *the* metric for corporate performance. While we all recognize the importance of other indicators such as market position, brands, intellectual capital, and long-term competitiveness, the bias is toward using a simple quantitative indicator that is easily compared period to period and across companies. And because EPS growth is an important driver of near-term share price improvement, managers are biased against investments that will compromise near-term EPS. Many decide instead to use the excess cash on the balance sheet to buy back the company's stock under the guise of "returning money to shareholders." But although contracting the number of shares pumps up earnings per share, sometimes quite dramatically, it does nothing to enhance the underlying value of the enterprise and may even damage it by restricting the flow of cash available for investment in potentially disruptive products and business models. Indeed, some have fingered share-price-based incentive compensation packages as a key driver of the share price manipulation that captured so many business headlines in the early 2000s.

The myopic focus on EPS is not just about the money. CEOs and corporate managers who are more concerned with their reputations than with amassing more wealth also focus on stock price and short-term performance measures such as quarterly earnings. They know that, to a large extent, others' perception of their success is tied up in those numbers, leading to a self-reinforcing cycle of obsession. This behavior cycle is amplified when there is an "earnings surprise." Equity prices over the short term respond positively to upside earnings surprises (and negatively to downside surprises), so investors have no incentive to look at rational measures of long-term performance. To the contrary, they are rewarded for going with the market's short-term model.

The active leveraged buyout market has further reinforced the focus on EPS. Companies that are viewed as having failed to maximize value, as evidenced by a lagging share price, are vulnerable to overtures from outsiders, including corporate raiders or hedge funds that seek to increase their near-term stock price by putting a company into play or by replacing the CEO. Thus, while the past two decades have witnessed a dramatic increase in the proportion of CEO compensation tied to stock price—and a breathtaking increase in CEO compensation overall—they have witnessed a concomitant decrease in the average tenure of CEOs. Whether you believe that CEOs are most motivated by the carrot (major increases in compensation and wealth) or the stick (the threat of the company being sold or of being replaced), you should not be surprised to find so many CEOs focused on current earnings per share as the best predictor of stock price, sometimes to the exclusion of anything else. One study even showed that senior executives were routinely willing to sacrifice long-term shareholder value to meet earnings expectations or to smooth reported earnings.

We suspect that the principal-agent theory is misapplied. Most traditional principals—by which we mean shareholders—don't themselves have incentives to watch out for the long-term health of a company. Over 90% of the shares of publicly traded companies in the United States are held in the portfolios of mutual funds, pension funds, and hedge funds. The average holding period for stocks in these portfolios is less than 10 months—leading us to prefer the term "share owner" as a more accurate description than "shareholder." As for agents, we believe that most executives work tirelessly, throwing their hearts and minds into their jobs, not because they are paid an incentive to do so but because they love what they do. Tying executive compensation to stock prices, therefore, does not affect the intensity or energy or intelligence with which executives perform. But it does direct their efforts toward activities whose impact can be felt within the holding horizon of the typical share owner and within the measurement horizon of the incentive—both of which are less than one year.

Ironically, most so-called principals today are themselves agents—agents of other people's mutual funds, investment portfolios, endowments, and retirement programs. For these agents, the enterprise in which they are investing has no inherent interest or value beyond providing a platform for improving the short-term financial metric by which their fund's performance is measured and their own compensation is determined. And, in a final grand but sad irony, the real principals (the people who put their money into mutual funds and pension plans, sometimes through yet another layer of agents) are frequently the very individuals whose long-term employment is jeopardized when the focus on short-term EPS acts to restrict investments in innovative growth opportunities. We suggest that the principal-agent theory is obsolete in this context. What we really have is an *agent-agent* problem, where the desires and goals of the agent for the share owners compete with the desires and goals of the agents running the company. The incentives are still misaligned, but managers should not capitulate on the basis of an obsolete paradigm.

## Processes That Support (or Sabotage) Innovation

As we have seen, managers in established corporations use analytical methods that make innovation investments extremely difficult to justify. As it happens, the most common system for green-lighting investment projects only reinforces the flaws inherent in the tools and dogmas discussed earlier.

## Stage-gate innovation

Most established companies start by considering a broad range of possible innovations; they winnow out the less viable ideas, step by step, until only the most promising ones remain. Most such processes include three stages: feasibility, development, and launch. The stages are separated by stage gates: review meetings at which project teams report to senior managers what they've accomplished. On the basis of this progress and the project's potential, the gatekeepers approve the passage of the initiative into the next phase, return it to the previous stage for more work, or kill it.

Many marketers and engineers regard the stage-gate development process with disdain. Why? Because the key decision criteria at each gate are the size of projected revenues and profits from the product and the associated risks. Revenues from products that incrementally improve upon those the company is currently selling can be credibly quantified. But proposals to create growth by exploiting potentially disruptive technologies, products, or business models can't be bolstered by hard numbers. Their markets are initially small, and substantial revenues generally don't materialize for several years. When these projects are pitted against incremental sustaining innovations in the battle for funding, the incremental ones sail through while the seemingly riskier ones get delayed or die.

The process itself has two serious drawbacks. First, project teams generally know how good the projections (such as NPV) need to look in order to win funding, and it takes only nanoseconds to tweak an assumption and run another full scenario to get a faltering project over the hurdle rate. If, as is often the case, there are eight to 10 assumptions underpinning the financial model, changing only a few of them by a mere 2% or 3% each may do the trick. It is then difficult for the senior managers who sit as gatekeepers to even discern which are the salient assumptions, let alone judge whether they are realistic.

The second drawback is that the stage-gate system assumes that the proposed strategy is the right strategy. Once an innovation has been approved, developed, and launched, all that remains is skillful execution. If, after launch, a product falls seriously short of the projections (and 75% of them do), it is canceled. The problem is that, except in the case of incremental innovations, the right strategy—especially which job the customer wants done—cannot be completely known in advance. It must emerge and then be refined.

The stage-gate system is not suited to the task of assessing innovations whose purpose is to build new growth businesses, but most companies continue to follow it simply because they see no alternative.

### Discovery-driven planning

Happily, though, there are alternative systems specifically designed to support intelligent investments in future growth. One such process, which Rita Gunther McGrath and Ian MacMillan call *discovery-driven planning*, has the potential to greatly improve the success rate. Discovery-driven planning essentially reverses the sequence of some of the steps in the stage-gate process. Its logic is elegantly simple. If the project teams all know how good the numbers need to look in order to win funding, why go through the charade of making and revising assumptions in order to fabricate an acceptable set of numbers? Why not just put the minimally acceptable revenue, income, and cash flow statement as the standard first page of the gate documents? The second page can then raise the critical issues: "Okay. So we all know this is how good the numbers need to look. What set of assumptions must prove true in order for these numbers to materialize?" The project team creates from that analysis an assumptions checklist—a list of things that need to prove true for the project to succeed. The items on the checklist are rank-ordered, with the deal killers and the assumptions that can be tested with little expense toward the top. McGrath and MacMillan call this a "reverse income statement."

When a project enters a new stage, the assumptions checklist is used as the basis of the project plan for that stage. This is not a plan to execute, however. It is a plan to *learn*—to test as quickly and at as low a cost as possible whether the assumptions upon which success is predicated are actually valid. If a critical assumption proves not to be valid, the project team must revise its strategy until the assumptions upon which it is built are all plausible. If no set of plausible assumptions will support the case for success, the project is killed.

Traditional stage-gate planning obfuscates the assumptions and shines the light on the financial projections. But there is no need to focus the analytical spotlight on the numbers, because the desirability of attractive numbers has never been the question. Discovery-driven planning shines a spotlight on the place where senior management needs illumination—the assumptions that constitute the key uncertainties. More often than not, failure in innovation is rooted in not having asked an important question, rather than in having arrived at an incorrect answer.

Today, processes like discovery-driven planning are more commonly used in entrepreneurial settings than in the large corporations that desperately need them. We hope that by recounting the strengths of one such system we'll persuade established corporations to reassess how they make decisions about investment projects.

---

We keep rediscovering that the root reason for established companies' failure to innovate is that managers don't have good tools to help them understand markets, build brands, find customers, select employees, organize teams, and develop strategy. Some of the tools typically used for financial analysis, and decision making about investments, distort the value, importance, and likelihood of success of investments in innovation. There's a better way for management teams to grow their companies. But they will need the courage to challenge some of the paradigms of financial analysis and the willingness to develop alternative methodologies.

**Originally published in January 2008. Reprint R0801F**

# About the Contributors

**LANCE A. BETTENCOURT** is a founding partner at Service 360 Partners.

**CLAYTON M. CHRISTENSEN** is the Kim B. Clark Professor of Business Administration at Harvard Business School and the world's foremost authority on disruptive innovation.

**GEORGE S. DAY** is the Geoffrey T. Boisi Professor and a codirector of the Mack Center for Technological Innovation at the University of Pennsylvania's Wharton School.

**PETER F. DRUCKER** the was the Marie Rankin Clarke Professor of Social Science and Management at Claremont Graduate University.

**VIJAY GOVINDARAJAN** is the Earl C. Daum 1924 Professor of International Business at the Tuck School of Business at Dartmouth.

**JEFFREY R. IMMELT,** chairman and CEO of GE, heads President Obama's Council on Jobs and Competitiveness.

**ROSABETH MOSS KANTER** is the Ernest L. Arbuckle Professor of Business Administration at Harvard Business School.

**STEPHEN P. KAUFMAN,** a senior lecturer at Harvard Business School, is the retired chairman and CEO of Arrow Electronics.

**IAN C. MACMILLAN** the Dhirubhai Ambani Professor of Innovation and Entrepreneurship at the University of Pennsylvania's Wharton School.

**ROGER L. MARTIN** is dean of the University of Toronto's Rotman School of Management.

**RITA GUNTHER MCGRATH** is a professor at Columbia University's Graduate School of Business.

**DONALD REINERTSEN** is president of Reinertsen & Associates, a consulting firm in Redondo Beach, California.

**WILLY C. SHIH** is a professor of management practice at Harvard Business School. He held executive positions at IBM, Silicon Graphics, and Kodak.

**STEFAN THOMKE** is the William Barclay Harding Professor of Business Administration at Harvard Business School.

**CHRIS TRIMBLE** is on the faculty at the Tuck School of Business at Dartmouth.

**ANTHONY W. ULWICK** is the founder and Chief Innovation Officer of Strategyn.

# Index

# Smart advice and inspiration from a source you trust.

Whether you need help tackling today's most urgent work challenge or shaping your organization's strategy for the future, *Harvard Business Review* has got you covered.

## HBR Guides Series

### HOW-TO ESSENTIALS FROM LEADING EXPERTS

HBR Guide to Better Business Writing
HBR Guide to Finance Basics for Managers
HBR Guide to Getting the Right Work Done
HBR Guide to Managing Up and Across
HBR Guide to Persuasive Presentations
HBR Guide to Project Management

## HBR's 10 Must Reads Series

### IF YOU READ NOTHING ELSE, READ THESE DEFINITIVE ARTICLES FROM HARVARD BUSINESS REVIEW

HBR's 10 Must Reads on Change Management
HBR's 10 Must Reads on Leadership
HBR's 10 Must Reads on Managing People
HBR's 10 Must Reads on Managing Yourself
HBR's 10 Must Reads on Strategy
HBR's 10 Must Reads: The Essentials

**Buy for your team, clients, or event.**
**Visit our site for quantity discount rates.**

hbr.org/books/direct-and-bulk-sales